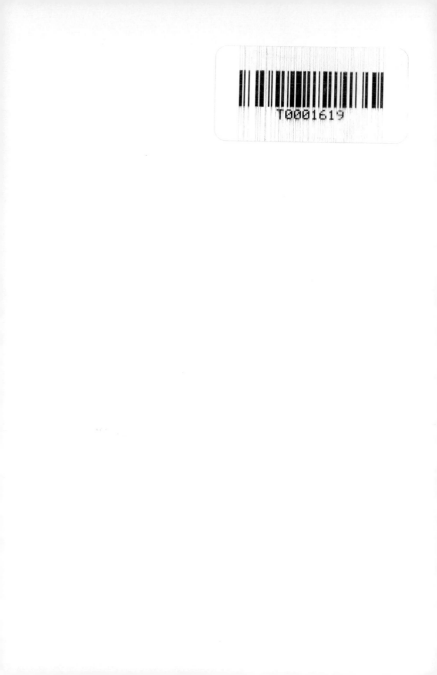

when the people pray

When the People Pray

An Invitation to Intercede for Your Pastor and Revive Your Church

thom s. rainer

TYNDALE
MOMENTUM®

A Tyndale nonfiction imprint

To pastors, God's servants:

We care for you.

We love you.

We pray for you.

Contents

A Brief Word to Church Members

YOU HAVE THIS BOOK IN YOUR HANDS FOR A REASON.

It is my prayer that this book and your decision to read it are a divine intersection. You see, if you really take this plan seriously and pray for your pastor for the next thirty days, you could see your church transformed.

I'm serious.

Your pastor has been called to lead your church spiritually. But your pastor is also up against a lot of battles, a multitude of expectations, and the constant nagging of doubts. Your pastor is in a spiritual battle. In fact, your pastor is being challenged daily by the enemy the Bible calls the devil.

Read the following verse carefully. Read it prayerfully:

Stay alert! Watch out for your great enemy, the devil. He prowls around like a roaring lion, looking for someone to devour.

1 PETER 5:8

This passage is applicable to all Christians, but it especially has meaning for pastors. If the enemy can distract, discourage, and disengage the pastors, the entire church suffers.

So what is *your* role? You are to "stay alert." You are to encourage your pastor. You are to minister to your pastor. Even more, you are to pray for your pastor.

Do you realize the importance of what you can do in God's power through prayer? As you pray for your pastor, you are not only praying for one person to be empowered; you are praying for an entire church to be empowered. As churches around the world are empowered, a revolution takes place in the heavenly realms. Indeed, a spiritual awakening could break out.

In many ways, my initial statement is an *under*statement. As you pray for your pastor, not only will you see your pastor and church transformed, but you could begin to see the *world* transformed.

The plan is simple and straightforward. Set aside thirty minutes per day for the next thirty days. Read and reflect on each day's challenge in the pages that follow and *pray for your pastor*.

I'm not suggesting you stop praying for your pastor at the end of thirty days. Rather, I'm encouraging you to *start* praying for your pastor now and make it a regular practice in your life from here on. This book is a catalyst. A starting point. It is not the grand finale.

Imagine you are about to embark on a journey that will change the world. You don't even need to imagine it. Just start praying daily and see what God will do—greater things than you can even "ask or think" (Ephesians 3:20).

As you pray for your pastor, I hope many others in your church will join you. I pray that your church will assemble an army to fight in this spiritual warfare. It is my fervent prayer that church members around the world will begin praying for their pastors more than ever.

Thank you for your willingness to take on this marvelous task and challenge. Stick with it. Give it the full thirty days and see what God will do.

See what God will do for your pastor.

See what God will do for your church.

And, yes, see what God will do in your own life.

And now, let us pray.

A Brief Word to Pastors

PASTORS, MAY I TELL YOU A STORY?

Many years ago, I pastored a difficult church. It was my third pastorate, but I had never before experienced the types of challenges that confronted me every day in this church. These challenges were not uncommon to pastors—critics, misunderstandings and misrepresentations, power groups, and a severe case of apathy among the flock—but it was the first time I had encountered such difficulties.

To be clear, I shared in the blame. I often responded poorly. I had my own attitude problem. And I could have used an extra measure of humility. Still, the church was difficult, and I really struggled. Not only did I have days when I wondered if I should stay at the church, but I sometimes wondered whether I should stay in vocational ministry.

Have you been there? I think we've all been there.

One Sunday morning, I was especially discouraged. As I walked to the pulpit, I did not feel like preaching. But somehow, by the grace of God, I made it through my sermon. At the conclusion of the service, I made some extemporaneous statements that I later wondered if I would regret. To the best of my memory, here is what I told the congregation:

> Folks, though it could be a risk, I want to be vulnerable and transparent with you. I am struggling. I am struggling as your pastor. I even had difficulty preaching today. I don't need to share all the reasons for my struggles; I know, above all, it's a spiritual battle. But at the risk of being presumptuous, could I ask something of you? Even if only a few of you are willing, it could make a huge difference for me. Will you commit to pray for me every day? Even if it's just a couple of minutes, will you pray for my ministry and for me? I know it's a big request, but I need prayers more than ever. I'm sorry to burden you with my own situation, but I really do need help, God's help. Thank you for any help you can give me.

Within two days, more than one hundred members of the church told me they had committed to pray for me daily. I was told many more were also involved. One of the larger contingents said they had committed to pray for me for one minute at noon every day, wherever they were and whatever they were doing.

I wept at their response. I still get teary-eyed thinking about it today.

I was transformed. Our church was transformed.

The power of prayer was at work.

Why do I tell you this story? It's simple. Like many pastors, you may be reluctant to ask your church members for help—and especially to pray for you. After all, you're supposed to be the strong spiritual leader in the church. Can you really afford to be that vulnerable?

Yes, you can. In fact, you can't afford *not* to be that vulnerable. You need to let go of any uncertainty or pride that hinders you from asking. You could be holding back something significant from taking place in your church. Yes, you could be hindering your own ministry.

After forty years of ministry, fellow pastor, I have learned a few things. I can be fiercely stubborn, too stubborn for my own good. But when I have asked and given permission for God's people to pray for me, I have seen many incredible things happen. I have seen miracles.

It's time. It's time for you to let go—of your fear, your pride, your reticence—and ask the members of your church to pray for you. Give them this book. Ask them to pray. See what God can do.

The apostle Paul asked for prayer. Why won't you?

Dear brothers and sisters, I urge you in the name of our Lord Jesus Christ to join in my struggle by praying to God for me. Do this because of your love for me, given to you by the Holy Spirit.

ROMANS 15:30

God

MOST CHURCH MEMBERS view pastors as people with a vibrant relationship with God. Indeed, it is true for most pastors most of the time.

But it is not true for all pastors all of the time.

Pastors have lapses.

Pastors can have misplaced priorities.

Pastors can get frustrated with all the demands placed on them.

Today is the first day of thirty that you will be praying for your pastor. Because it is the beginning, it is the most important day. It's also the most important day because you are praying for your pastor's relationship with God.

Every pastor who is transparent will tell you about struggles. Though it's a cliché to say that pastors are human, they really do wrestle with all the same issues you do. They get discouraged. They have doubts. They face temptation and succumb to sin.

Though I encourage you to admire your pastor and have the utmost respect for your pastor, do not put him on a pedestal. Do not make him something he is not. If you do, you will see little need to pray for your pastor. If pastors had perfect strength and wisdom, they wouldn't need your prayers. But pastors are not perfect, and they do need your prayers.

Your pastor needs regular prayers for a firm and unwavering commitment and relationship with God. Your pastor is powerless unless that strength comes from God.

> Stay on the path that the LORD your God has commanded you to follow. Then you will live long and prosperous lives in the land you are about to enter and occupy.
> DEUTERONOMY 5:33

Reflection

The room was filled with pastors, probably fifty or more. They had come to learn how to lead their churches and reach their communities more effectively. They came to the conference with high expectations.

Of course, we don't know what was in the minds and hearts of all the pastors. But we know about some of them.

Early in the conference, one pastor said he was there because his church had been in a slow but steady decline for six years. He had tried everything to no avail. He was frustrated. At times, he was despondent. He admitted to everyone in the room that he'd even had moments where he questioned his calling and competency.

God used that pastor's level of transparency to encourage some of the other pastors to be more transparent and more vulnerable.

Two pastors admitted they had the same questions and concerns as the first pastor. One confessed that his life had become spiritually dry. He didn't know how he could lead his church if he was not growing spiritually himself.

The conference took a dramatic turn as the keynote speaker was about to present his message. God was clearly moving, and the speaker took the cue. He did not want to quench the work of the Spirit.

"Let's take a few minutes to pray before we get into today's content," he said to the gathered pastors. He opened the floor to anyone who wanted to voice a prayer.

Those "few minutes" turned into an hour. Pastors began praying for a restored relationship with God. Some confessed that their busyness had caused them to neglect their time with God. A few were sobbing quietly, unable to speak.

These pastors had come with their notebooks, expecting some practical guidance on leading their churches to growth. But the real issue was their need to grow in their own relationship with God.

Later, one of the pastors shared with the speaker what had happened with him during this time.

"I realized I could not begin to lead my church when I was running on empty myself," he admitted. "I had to let God deal with me and my relationship with him first. I know I'm not alone when I describe myself as a pastor who needs God."

Indeed, that pastor is not alone. Many pastors admit they have let the demands of church life and leadership impinge on their relationship with God. Your pastor likely has these moments as well. As you take this journey for the next thirty days, you will discover the incredible expectations placed on pastors. You will also discover their struggles and challenges.

If you read the words closely, you will also discover that, more than anything else, pastors need a vibrant and deep relationship with God. They cannot lead unless they are first filled.

It's time for that filling to take place.

It's time we church members prayed for our pastors.

And the first item on our list is to pray for their ongoing relationship with God.

Praying for My Pastor

God, I pray first that my pastor would walk with you more closely and know you more deeply.

Sometimes I'm not aware of the demands placed on pastors. I do not fully grasp the scope and range of expectations coming from so many different church members. Pastors are often expected to be everywhere and to know everything.

I pray for my pastor to know when to slow down and spend time with you, Lord. Busyness cannot replace a relationship with you. Pastors cannot please everyone, but they must always strive to please you.

Help me to see the life of my pastor more clearly. Help me to understand his needs and struggles so I can pray more diligently. Teach me to have a heart of compassion, empathy, and awareness.

Above all, remind me to pray for my pastor to have a dynamic relationship with you. Pastors can't lead others until they are first led by you, God.

Lord, please place my pastor in a posture to know you better.

Only then can my pastor be the leader of this church you have molded and shaped.

In Jesus' name,

Amen.

Wisdom

MOST PEOPLE SIMPLY HAVE NO IDEA of the number of decisions a pastor has to make in the course of a day.

Some are not earth-shattering decisions. Do we schedule the men's event for 7:00 p.m. or 7:30 p.m.? What is the schedule for the staff's days off for Christmas? How many chairs do we need now that we have removed the pews? Should I attend the community pastors' meeting every week?

Of course, even seemingly inconsequential events can create challenges. One pastor said the decision to move from pews to chairs became a major conflict in his church. He had no preference; he just wanted the church to decide and get the work done. But it was not that easy. There were strong feelings on both sides. Arguments ensued. Conflict became the dominant attitude.

When the pastor was deciding how many chairs to purchase to replace the pews, the conflict resurfaced. The pew advocates were still angry.

Then there are decisions that are really life changing. "My husband had an affair; do I leave him or give him another chance?" Most pastors will get that question at some point in their ministry. Yet another pastor shared that a terminally ill man inquired whether it was okay to ask the medical personnel to withhold further treatment. He was tired and ready to die.

Then there were pastors who strongly disagreed with changes in their denomination's doctrine. Should they lead their churches out of the denomination or let the issue lie? They were torn. They needed wisdom.

In the course of a week, most pastors make a dozen or more decisions. Some are small. Some are significant. Some are quickly forgotten. Some have an impact for a lifetime.

All of them require wisdom.

> The wisdom from above is first of all pure. It is also peace loving, gentle at all times, and willing to yield to others. It is full of mercy and the fruit of good deeds. It shows no favoritism and is always sincere.
> JAMES 3:17

Reflection

Alice, the church treasurer, was a godly woman. She had served the church faithfully in that role for fourteen years. She was also an accomplished certified public accountant with a thriving practice.

She loved the Lord. She loved her church. She loved her pastor. And she did not want to bring him the news she was about to deliver. Her pastor, Mark, was a faithful servant. He had led the church well for ten years, a tenure longer than any pastor's in the previous fifty years at the church.

But Mark and the church had an uphill challenge. Their small community had been steadily losing population for almost two decades, and the past two years had been especially difficult. The largest industry in town had finally closed. It had been declining for years, so the ultimate shutdown was not really a surprise. Still, the finality of the closing was painful.

As a result of the plant closure, four families in the church moved to find work elsewhere. Three of those four families had been among the most faithful givers in the congregation. For years, the church had been dealing with a slightly declining budget, but adjustments had been made along the way. Some cuts had been painful, but the congregation had accepted them. But now the situation had become dire.

Alice and Mark met in a big conference room with spacious windows to the hallway. Mark liked to be visible when he met with people, though the room offered conversational privacy.

Mark knew Alice well. He originally thought the meeting would be another review of the church's budget and finances. He was not unaware of the budgetary crunch, but the church had always found a way to make cuts here and there. The moment he saw Alice's face, however, he knew this conversation wouldn't be like the others.

After a brief greeting, he waited for Alice to speak.

"This conversation isn't easy," she said with a quiver in her voice. "I've looked over our finances again and again, but there is no way around it. The closing of the Harrison Company plant has hurt the town and the church. We no longer have any places to make small adjustments."

"So what do we do?" Mark asked. Even as the words left his mouth, he knew he didn't want to hear the answer.

"Mark, we have to cut one of our three full-time ministers," Alice responded soberly. "We've already moved everyone we can to part-time, and now we have to make deeper cuts."

"Are there no other options?" Mark asked semi-rhetorically.

"No, I'm sorry," Alice said softly. "Other than you, we have only Becca and Dan. One of them will have to be let go. You need to decide."

You need to decide. Those four words reverberated in Mark's mind. *Why?* he wondered. *Why do I have to decide?*

Both Becca and Dan were valuable church staff members. They were fiercely loyal to their pastor. They worked sacrificially for the church. And they both had families to support.

You need to decide.

Seminary had not prepared Mark for moments like this. Indeed, many of the decisions he had to make had never been mentioned in his theological training.

He had two weeks before the annual budget process began. He needed to make a decision. Above all, though, he needed wisdom.

Praying for My Pastor

I begin this prayer for my pastor, Lord, with a confession.

Too often, I take my pastor for granted.

Too often, I don't consider all the decisions a pastor has to make. Too often, I assume that my pastor has received all the training necessary to lead and serve our church. Too often, I think my pastor has all the answers—or should.

Forgive me for not having greater empathy and compassion for my pastor, who confronts so many challenges every day.

Right now, God, I pray for wisdom for my pastor. I pray for all pastors who are facing difficult decisions today. Please, Lord, give them clarity of thought and boldness backed by wisdom.

I pray that my pastor will never feel alone when dealing with difficult decisions and challenges. May my pastor feel your presence, recognize your power, and know your wisdom.

In Jesus' name,

Amen.

Family

IT IS A VERSE IN THE BIBLE that causes anxiety for many pastors.

Paul writes to his young protégé, Timothy, to provide clarity on a number of items, particularly the qualifications for church leaders. He tells Timothy that leaders must be above reproach, and married leaders must be faithful spouses. They must demonstrate self-control. They must live wisely. They must have a good reputation. They must be hospitable. They must be able to teach. They cannot drink heavily or be violent. They must be gentle and not quarrelsome. And they mustn't have a love for money.

Whew.

Most pastors are able to meet the qualifications in 1 Timothy 3:1-3. But when they read verses 4 and 5, it makes them a bit uncomfortable. Paul says very clearly that church leaders must lead their own families well before they can lead God's church.

The challenge for every pastor is that no one has a perfect family. If the pastor's kids get a bit rowdy or struggle with temptation or have problems at school, does that disqualify the pastor from ministry? If a teenage PK goes through a period of rebellion, does it mean the pastor must step down from leadership?

Paul was obviously speaking about neglect of duty. He didn't mean that an act of imperfection would disqualify a pastor.

Still, many pastors feel enormous pressure to lead their families well. They are on call 24/7 for the church, and they worry that their families suffer from the demands of the job. They wonder whether they can really lead both their families and their churches well.

We not only must pray for our pastor's leadership at home; we must pray for his family, as well. Yes, wives and children feel the pressure too. They are in a fishbowl, under scrutiny by the congregation.

Pray for your pastor as he leads his family. Pray for each family member by name.

> If a man cannot manage his own household, how can he take care of God's church?
>
> 1 TIMOTHY 3:5

Reflection

Eleven-year-old Micah was a good kid. He was obedient to his parents most of the time, yet he was always active. "Micah came out of the womb kicking and screaming," his father, Jeff, shared, "and he hasn't slowed down since." Jeff is the pastor of a normative-size church in Texas.

Jeff had received more than one complaint from a church member about Micah running full speed in the worship venue after services were over. On several occasions, he had yielded to the temptation to bang on the drums on the stage. One particular incident caused the chairman of the deacon board to lodge his own complaint.

"I love my son so much," Jeff quickly affirmed. "I don't think of him as rebellious or disobedient, but maybe I have too much parental bias." Jeff paused for a moment. "Still, I have to admit that the complaints about his hyperactivity are increasing. I am also in my third year as pastor, so I'm well past the honeymoon stage. I'm getting a lot more complaints in general, not just about Micah."

Jeff could not deny that Micah was becoming more rambunctious. And lately, he had become argumentative, as well. Some of it, Jeff reasoned, could be preadolescence. But at eleven years old, Micah was no longer "just a kid." He should be able to control himself.

Jeff wondered what he would do if Micah's situation did not improve. How much longer could he keep telling church members that he would take care of his son? Even more, how much longer would the church members put up with the problem? The situation at the church seemed fragile. It seemed that many of the members were just looking for excuses to blame the pastor for almost anything.

The challenge with his son was a challenge that many parents faced. But was it a challenge that should make him consider leaving the church? Had it gotten to the point where he was neglecting his first ministry—his family—for others in the church? Or, as some members suggested, was he neglecting his pastoral ministry because he had to give so much attention to his son?

Jeff and his wife prayed every night about this issue. They did not want to abandon those they had been called to serve. But they knew that Micah came first. If they needed to make a change, they were willing.

Jeff was torn. He wanted to stay at his church, but he was not sure that would even be an option in the near future. What should he do?

Praying for My Pastor

Lord, please hear my prayer for my pastor.

So many responsibilities and expectations are placed on him. He is expected to be at meetings, events, and visits at the hospital and in members' homes.

He has to prepare sermons and teach small groups. He must be a visionary, a shepherd, an administrator, and a counselor all in one.

My pastor has a family who needs him first. They are his first line of ministry in the church, but they are often relegated to the end of the line. I know that frustrates and hurts my pastor. Please give him discernment to know how to set the right priorities.

And be with my pastor's family. Be their shepherd and comforter when the pastor is away. Help them to love your church even when the church is not loving toward them.

Thank you, Lord, for looking after our pastor and his family. They need your strength and wisdom more than ever.

In Jesus' name,
Amen.

Preparation

"I WISH I HAD YOUR JOB, PASTOR. You only work one hour a week."

Certainly, most church members make such claims in jest. They know a pastor's workweek is not limited to one hour on Sunday morning. They know the pastor does more than preach a sermon once a week.

But even in jest, those barbs can be painful to pastors. First, they've heard the same line many times. The joke can get old and irksome. Second, pastors know that some church members believe there's a bit of truth in the joke, that pastors are only working when they're visible to the congregation. And most members have no idea how much time goes into preparing a sermon.

Many pastors spend fifteen to twenty-five hours per week preparing—studying the passage, taking notes, praying for wisdom and discernment, and working with interpretive resources and commentaries.

WHEN THE PEOPLE PRAY

The actual writing of a sermon can be laborious, whether it is written as a manuscript or an outline. Pastors want to deal with the text as it was originally communicated, but they also want to understand the ancient text in the context of the twenty-first century. And they must communicate in ways that will connect with their congregation, using illustrations and making applications.

Above all, pastors don't want their sermons to be the product of mere human ingenuity. They pray for God to speak through them (1 Peter 4:11). They seek God's blessing. They pray for God's anointing. They pray for those who will hear the message. They truly want to be vessels for the Holy Spirit.

That's just for one sermon. Once it's been preached, the process starts all over again. Every week. Every month. Every year.

> Preach the word of God. Be prepared, whether the time is favorable or not. Patiently correct, rebuke, and encourage your people with good teaching.
>
> 2 TIMOTHY 4:2

Reflection

Frank tried working at the church office when he prepared his sermons. In fact, he tried it for his first full year at the church before giving up. Initially, he did his sermon prep with his office door open. Both staff and church members would see him through the open door and begin a conversation. Frank did not want to be rude, so he engaged every time someone began to chat.

He knew after a while that something had to give. He was losing hours of precious study time to be a friendly guy to the members and the staff. He thought his sermons suffered as well.

His next step was to do his sermon study and preparation behind closed doors. That didn't work either. First, people would knock on the door and ask him if he was busy. Frank simply did not have the heart to tell them that, yes, he was indeed busy. The church receptionist/assistant was not helpful either. If anyone called the church office and asked if the pastor was in, she felt it was a matter of integrity to say yes and forward the call to Frank.

So Frank began working outside the office at various coffeehouses. It wasn't ideal; distractions abounded all around him. But he discovered an unwritten coffeehouse code: If you're working on your computer with earbuds in, you will not be disturbed. Though it was certainly not the best way to focus on study, it was his solution for a few months.

Very few church members, he realized, really understood all that went into the preparation of one sermon, especially if it was to be done well. The act of preaching was contingent on the power of prayer and the pastor's diligence in preparation.

Frank thought the ideal solution would be to prepare his sermons at home. His kids were in school or busy with other activities. His wife encouraged him to turn a small room in the house into a study and work at least one day a week from home preparing his message. But when Frank ran the idea by his deacons, they were unanimously opposed. How would it look, they reasoned, if the pastor was at home instead of at the church?

So Frank nixed the move home until 2020. Of course, that was the year of the COVID-19 pandemic. With the church offices and local coffeehouses closed, Frank and his staff had no choice but to work from home. In the early months of 2020, most of his sermons were for streaming services online. It was a period of significant change, and his sermon preparation time was clearly affected.

He finally went through with the build-out of a small office at his house. He brought home the necessary commentaries, Bibles, and other resources but found he could access most of what he needed from the internet anyway. He got into a rhythm of working from home. He found himself more productive than ever.

When the church began to regather in person, Frank kept doing his sermon preparation from home. He didn't even think to get the deacons' permission this time. And the deacons didn't seem to notice. Even now, Frank continues to work from home at least two days a week.

Praying for My Pastor

Lord, may your Holy Spirit not only empower my pastor to preach but also empower him to prepare his sermons with wisdom and insight.

Give him clarity of mind and heart as he works through the text and as he grasps not only its original intent but also how it applies to our lives today. Keep his mind focused and free from distractions.

Give him uninterrupted study time. May he be so deep in the Scripture and the preparation of the sermon that time flies and that he studies and writes unhindered. Let him not be exhausted by sermon preparation but energized by it. I pray that it will be a time he anticipates with joy each week.

It is my prayer, God, that our pastor would approach the time of sermon preparation each week with wonder and excitement.

May he preach his sermons with the confidence of one who is well prepared—but even more so as one who has been prepared by you.

In Jesus' name,

Amen.

Preaching

FOR SOME CHURCH MEMBERS, preaching is the essence of what a pastor does. Indeed, many pastors view their call to ministry as a call to preach. The weekly sermon is central. It is the key to the life and health of a church.

It is amazing to think about all that goes into one sermon. Certainly, there is the preparation process. Most pastors devote at least fifteen to twenty-five hours a week to writing their sermons.

There is also the planning of the rest of the worship time. Though the sermon is central, a typical weekend service includes music, prayer, announcements, and other acts of worship, such as Communion, baptisms, or testimonies. It can't be done haphazardly.

But there is something supernatural about the act of preaching. God works through the efforts of the pastor, who prepares a sermon using Spirit-inspired Scripture. Then, as the pastor preaches, God's Spirit works in the hearts of those who hear the sermon.

Think about how many lives have been changed through the preaching of God's Word. Think about how many people have seen their eternity changed through preaching. Think about how many marriages and families have been restored through preaching. Think about how many people have made commitments to serve God at a deeper level through preaching.

And think about how your own life has been shaped and changed through preaching.

Preaching. It's one of the most important facets of church life.

Indeed, it is vital to the health of the church.

We must pray for the ones who preach every week, both when they are preaching and during the week when they are preparing.

Preaching is just that important.

My message and my preaching were very plain. Rather than using clever and persuasive speeches, I relied only on the power of the Holy Spirit. I did this so you would trust not in human wisdom but in the power of God.

I CORINTHIANS 2:4-5

Reflection

Mateo absolutely loved to preach. It was the one time during the week when he had most of the members' attention. It was an opportunity to dig into the Bible. It was that remarkable moment each week when God's Word spoke to God's people through God's spokesman.

It was the center of his ministry.

It was his joy and his burden.

Mateo would admit that early in his ministry, he didn't fully

21

grasp the burden of preaching to his congregation. As he gained experience and matured, he realized more and more that he was a spokesman for God. He taught God's Word to his congregation.

"When I began to understand more fully what I was doing," Mateo told us, "I began to see clearly that the honor of preaching for God was also an enormous responsibility. Those who sit under my preaching every week are hearing, to use a bit of King James English, 'Thus saith the Lord.'"

That realization changed his approach to preaching.

"Right before I step up to the pulpit, I ask God to prepare me once again," Mateo confided. "I have learned I cannot preach for God in my own strength and power. I also pray for those who will hear my preaching. I am fallible, but God's Word is infallible. I must have God's wisdom before I preach."

Mateo is one of many pastors who have asked their congregations to pray for them while they are preaching.

"We have a rotation of three members at a time who pray for the worship services," he told us. "They can hear the service through speakers in the room. They are able to pray specifically for what is happening in real time. I know they are in fervent prayer while I preach."

Mateo paused for a moment. "Frankly, I can't imagine preaching without praying for my own sermon. And I can't imagine preaching without someone else praying for me while I preach. I know for a fact my ministry was transformed by the prayer ministry of our church."

He looked aside briefly and continued, "Think about it. Those twenty-five to fifty minutes when the pastor is preaching are likely the most transformational minutes in the world each week. Earth and heaven are moved when we preach. We often get caught up in the routine and take it for granted."

Mateo added in a measured voice, "We cannot and must not take preaching for granted. We pastors must preach with God's power. I pray that many church members will pray for the time of preaching as well. It's too important to neglect. It's just too important."

Praying for My Pastor

God, I ask that you empower my pastor every time he preaches. Let him be confident—not in himself, but in you as you work through him.

Give him the words you want him to share with us who hear his sermons every week. Take his preparation this week and transform it into a message that will transform us.

If he is weary, give him strength.

If he is distracted, give him focus.

If he is worried, give him assurance.

If he is hurting, give him comfort.

And for those who sit under his preaching, give us ears to hear. Let us be transformed by your Word as he preaches. Let us focus on what you would have us hear. As we pray for our pastor to be focused, may we be focused as well. May our attitude be one of discernment for this message for our own lives.

So, God, may we see the miracle of your Word communicated through your servant transforming your people every time he preaches. Then we will know we have heard from you again.

In Jesus' name,

Amen.

Criticism

HAVE YOU HEARD OF "DEATH BY A THOUSAND CUTS"?

The phrase originated with an ancient form of torture in China. In *lingchi*, which means "slow process" or "lingering death," victims were slowly and methodically cut to maximize their suffering until they were finished off with a stab to the heart or decapitation.

Today, the term refers to a series of negative events that, in the aggregate, result in a very bad outcome. A business, for example, can make a series of small bad decisions, none of which by itself would jeopardize the viability of the company. But the sum of bad decisions could result in bankruptcy.

Many pastors receive criticism regularly, if not daily. They could brush off any one of these comments, or even a few. But as criticism piles up, the cumulative weight of negativity sabotages the pastor's emotional and spiritual health. Many pastors have been rendered ineffective due to death by a thousand cutting remarks. Others have resigned from their churches.

Pastors need intercession in three major ways. First, they need prayer to withstand criticism. Second, they need church members to stand up for them and (if necessary) challenge and rebuke those who lob unwarranted criticism. Third, they need intercessions of encouragement. As one pastor shared with us, he began to believe he was as bad as his critics said because no other church members said otherwise.

A church full of critics will never be a healthy church, particularly if their criticism is aimed at the pastor.

> If you are always biting and devouring one another, watch out! Beware of destroying one another.
>
> GALATIANS 5:15

Reflection

Mike had very few real friends in the church. Most of his friendships were with other pastors and those he had gotten to know well in seminary many years earlier. He also considered his two brothers and his dad to be among his best friends.

He really felt blessed. Though he did not have close friends in the church, there were about a dozen men with whom he had strong relationships. He knew he could call on any one of them at any time.

Mike was in his fourth year at the church. His ministry there had started well, but things had gotten bumpy in year three. He tried to look honestly at himself to see what mistakes he'd made so he wouldn't make them again. Indeed, those who knew Mike saw him as a man of high emotional intelligence who would always look in the mirror first when dealing with problems. But as much as he thought and prayed about it, he couldn't isolate any one factor that had contributed to the growing negativity in the church.

When the criticism began to increase in frequency, Mike tried to manage the situation on his own. He knew that many pastors endured similar low points. He could get through it. But as the criticism became more intense, Mike grew weary. When he turned to his friends outside the church, they were supportive and offered some sage advice, but none of their proposed solutions or approaches ultimately helped.

Knowing he had to try something else, Mike decided to confide in and seek counsel from a trusted church member. He chose one of the three most respected people in the congregation, an elder named Marcus, who had been in the church for more than twenty years. Mike saw Marcus as a friend—not as close a friend as those he had outside the church, but still a steady and reliable relationship.

Marcus was a successful businessman, having started and grown his company to more than $20 million in revenue. Not only was he respected in the church, but he was admired in the business community as well.

The two men met in Marcus's office. Like many businesspeople, Marcus did not offer much small talk. Within a minute of the pastor's arrival, he said, "It has to be a pretty serious issue for you to make an hour-long appointment with me at my office. What's up, Mike?"

Mike explained the problem. He gave a quick overview of the steady and mounting criticism over the past two years. And he admitted he was weary, even thinking at times about leaving the church.

When Mike was done, Marcus stared at him for a few seconds, but it seemed like several minutes to Mike.

Finally, Marcus spoke. "Mike," he began. "I have to admit I'm stunned. You have every right to feel hurt and weary. But I'm stunned because I had no idea this stuff was going on. I felt like I had my ear to the ground about our church, but I totally missed this one."

Marcus paused for a minute and then continued, "I wonder how many pastors have situations like yours, where most of the members have no idea of the hurt their pastors are absorbing." He reflected further, "Members who love their pastors can't help if they don't know there is a problem. We have to get to work on this issue."

Praying for My Pastor

Lord, please give my pastor the strength to endure the criticism he receives. When the barbs seem unending, give him a gentle reminder that you are there for him.

In the midst of the criticism, give him both perspective and focus. Give him the perspective that far more members are for him than against him. Give him the focus to move forward on the things that really matter.

And, God, I ask you to mobilize and motivate us members to better support our pastor. He already has a group of critics. Raise up an army of defenders and encouragers.

Finally, work in the hearts of the critics. Convict them of a critical spirit where necessary, and open their eyes to all that our pastor does for them and our church. When they do offer feedback, may it be from a posture of love and brokenness. May they address issues of major importance rather than petty grievances and preferences.

May the critics become fewer in number as the encouragers grow into a multitude.

Thank you, Lord.

In Jesus' name,

Amen.

Conflict

MOST PASTORS receive criticism on a regular basis. Sometimes, however, there is negativity in the church that is not specifically directed at the pastor. It could be between opposing factions or the fallout from a power group in the church that seeks to control the congregation's ministries, money, and activities. Power groups can act as benevolent dictators or as pure bullies.

Though conflict in the church may not directly involve the pastor, he may take the conflict personally. After all, he has responsibility for spiritual leadership in the church. Unity in the church is absolutely necessary for the congregation to carry out its mission.

When church members are in conflict with one another, the church becomes inwardly focused. When a church focuses on itself, it can't reach outward to serve and reach others. Evangelism is thwarted, and the church stops ministering to the community.

One of the first recorded accounts of dissension and conflict in the church appears in Acts 6:1-7. The Greek-speaking believers in Jerusalem accused the Hebrew-speaking believers of giving preferential treatment to their own in the church's food ministry. Acts 6:1 describes the situation well: "As the believers rapidly multiplied, there were rumblings of discontent."

The context is clear. The church's evangelistic momentum was at risk because of internal conflict in the church. But the leaders of the church quickly addressed and resolved the problem before it could fester and hinder the mission of the church.

The results of dealing with the conflict positively and resolutely are recorded in Acts 6:7: "God's message continued to spread. The number of believers greatly increased in Jerusalem, and many of the Jewish priests were converted, too."

Conflict destroys unity. Disunity destroys the ministry of the church.

It is one of the pastor's greatest burdens, and common enough to prompt these words from the apostle Paul:

> I appeal to you, dear brothers and sisters, by the authority of our Lord Jesus Christ, to live in harmony with each other. Let there be no divisions in the church. Rather, be of one mind, united in thought and purpose.
>
> I CORINTHIANS 1:10

Reflection

It was not a good sign.

When Pastor Hayden became nervous and fearful, he had a clear physical indicator: His right hand would shake. It wasn't noticeable to most people, though his wife and children knew about it and a few close friends had noticed it. The tremors always felt more pronounced than they appeared, and Hayden could usually hide them. But he always felt them.

Hayden's main concern this time was that he genuinely dreaded the meeting he was about to attend. The tremors merely confirmed the angst he was feeling.

In ten minutes, he would walk into a room for the church's quarterly business meeting. The church's polity was congregational, and the bylaws gave a lot of authority to the members. To be honest, it gave too much authority to the members, who were asked to vote on even the minutest aspects of church life. Any time people have to vote on something, two sides inevitably rise up in opposition to one another.

This time, the vote would likely be on Hayden himself. He had been at the church for almost five years. Though he had experienced some conflict, nothing like this issue had ever arisen in his ministry.

Two months earlier, a staff member had been dismissed for moral failure. The church leaders had been gracious, and no details were released about the man's indiscretions for fear it would hurt his family. The church had also provided a generous severance.

But for several families in the church, the dismissed staff member had been "their guy." They were loyal to him to a fault. And he had been at the church longer than Hayden. Though the dismissal had come from a personnel committee, the fringe group blamed the pastor. He was the convenient target.

When Hayden walked into the room, his worst fears were realized. More people were in attendance than at a typical worship service. Members had come out of the woodwork for what promised to be a contentious gathering. In fact, some members were present who had not attended in years. Hayden didn't recognize at least a third of the crowd.

The staff member's supporters had done their homework. The bylaws gave church members authority to dismiss a pastor on the spot with a 60 percent majority vote of those present. When the meeting got to the agenda item of "other business," the group went into action. A motion and second were made to dismiss Hayden immediately.

The discussion got real ugly real fast. People shouted. False accusations were made. It was more of a mob action than a meeting. After nearly ninety minutes of verbal warfare, the vote was taken. The dissenting group fell far short of the needed 60 percent. The final count was 42 percent for dismissal.

But the damage was done. About a hundred people left the church shortly thereafter. The more reasonable church members were shell-shocked. Hayden wondered for weeks whether he could ever serve effectively as their pastor again. In fact, he wondered whether he could ever serve *anywhere* as a pastor again.

Praying for My Pastor

Lord, I pray for unity in the church. I remember your words in John 17:20-23, when you prayed for all believers to be as one:

> *I am praying not only for these disciples but also for all who will ever believe in me through their message. I pray that they will all be one, just as you and I are one—as you are in me, Father, and I am in you. And may they be in us so that the world will believe you sent me. I have given them the glory you gave me, so they may be one as we are one. I am in them and*

you are in me. May they experience such perfect unity that the world will know that you sent me and that you love them as much as you love me.

God, I pray for my pastor as he attempts to lead our church in greater unity. It is difficult to be a servant leader in a church under any circumstance. It is almost impossible to lead when a church is fractured and fighting.

Thank you, Father, for being the source and model of unity. May we know your presence more fully in our church.

In Jesus' name,

Amen.

DAY 8

Prayer

CHURCH MEMBERS are often surprised when they find out that many pastors struggle with their personal prayer life. After all, they are the spiritual leaders of the church. Shouldn't they have this prayer discipline down?

It is good to reflect at times on the humanity of pastors. They have many great attributes. Most pastors truly love their church members unconditionally and sacrificially. Most have made significant sacrifices to prepare to become pastors. In many ways, it is right to look up to pastors.

But they are still human.

Don't put them on a pedestal. Don't see them as impervious to pain. And don't think they are perfect in their practice of spiritual disciplines.

Many pastors struggle to have a consistent personal prayer life. We're all busy, and everyone has the challenge of managing priorities, but the expectations placed on a pastor are usually multiplied by the number of church members. Particularly, they are expected to be on call 24/7/365. For certain, they must be present when a member's son has been in a tragic automobile accident. For sure, they need to be by the side of people who are fading from this life but want to know about eternal life.

Still, some of the expectations in the realm of the mundane—attendance at committee meetings, settling petty differences between church members, running point on facility maintenance, managing the church calendar—can tip the balance toward overload and squeeze out other, more important concerns.

Indeed, the time demands on a pastor are many. It is not unusual for the pastor's prayer life to suffer as a result. The most important priority is often pushed aside—or at least impinged upon—by the tyranny of the urgent.

We should pray for our pastors' prayer lives. And we should do all we can to make sure they have the space and time to be people of prayer.

> Keep watch and pray, so that you will not give in to
> temptation. For the spirit is willing, but the body is weak.
> MATTHEW 26:41

Reflection

It can really be a blessing when a pastor has a good friend in his congregation. Pastors don't often have real friends among their membership. After all, pastors are called to serve and care for the flock. The sheep are not typically responsible for caring for the shepherd. It's mostly a one-way relationship.

Occasionally, however, a pastor will discover the kind of friend who will give as well as receive. The kind of friend who always has a word of encouragement and is also willing to offer words of caution or even rebuke. A true friend always operates from a posture of love.

Such friends are rare. They should be treated as the treasures they are.

Franco and Marion are best friends. They are in the same church. Franco is the pastor, and Marion is a physician who has held several leadership positions in the church.

Neither one can remember the point where they knew they were best friends. As Marion said, "We didn't declare the moment, nor did we plan to become best friends. It just kind of happened. I guess that's the way most good friendships evolve."

Franco concurred: "I've been at the church for eight years, and I can't remember when our friendship became the relationship it is today."

Both men have several stories that affirm the depth of their relationship, but the one they seem to remember most quickly and clearly was related to Franco's prayer life.

"Yeah," Marion recalled, "I just kept reading in the Bible where leaders must find time to pray. I heard stories of how pastors are under spiritual attack. I decided to ask Franco about his own prayer life."

"Well, you asked in your usual no-nonsense way," Franco responded with a smile. "You walked into my office and asked me straight out. No prefatory comments. No greeting. No context. Just the question."

"At least I was honest," Marion replied with a similar wry smile.

"Franco admitted his personal prayer life was suffering. I knew we had to get to work."

Marion and Franco met with the part-time assistant who kept Franco's calendar. They blocked off an hour a day for prayer. The assistant agreed not to interrupt that time unless it was a true emergency.

When Franco admitted he had trouble focusing during his prayer times, Marion got him a prayer journal so he could write many of his prayers.

Marion, of course, would also hold him accountable. He wouldn't pry into the privacy of the prayer journal, but he would ask Franco on a regular basis how his prayer life was going.

"Marion is never judgmental when he asks me about my prayer life," Franco said with conviction. "I know it is always out of love and friendship."

Marion also enlisted seven other church members to pray for Franco every day. He asked them only to commit to a few minutes a day but to be consistent. They were to pray for their pastor however they felt led, but Marion asked them also to pray for the pastor's personal prayer life.

"My ministry has never been stronger," Franco said with enthusiasm. "And I know it's because I am depending less on my own power and strength and more on God's. That's what prayer will do."

Franco paused for a moment and then added, "By the way, I have discovered the definition of a true friend. It is someone who cares so much for you that he wants you to be as close to God as possible."

Praying for My Pastor

Lord, make my pastor a man of prayer.

Show him how to take time out of each day to spend with you. Let it be a priority and passion of his life. Help him to see there are few things more important in his life and ministry than prayer.

Lord, my pastor has so many responsibilities. He carries so many burdens. Lift those burdens from him even as you give him strength. Let him see that he can do anything through you and nothing apart from you.

And help me, I pray, to be both an encourager and an intercessor for my pastor. As I pray for him, may one of my most fervent prayers be for him to have a dynamic prayer life with you. Convict other church members to pray for our pastor as well.

We know that as a person of prayer, our pastor will have all he needs as he shepherds this church. Then, and only then, can he lead this church well.

In Jesus' name,
Amen.

Word

WHEN THE FIRST CHURCH in Jerusalem met with conflict over "the daily distribution of food" to the widows in the congregation, "there were rumblings of discontent" (Acts 6:1).

We typically (and rightly) focus on the actions the apostles took to solve the problem. They "called a meeting of all the believers" (Acts 6:2). They asked the people to appoint seven men to take responsibility for the food distribution (Acts 6:3). And they affirmed the ministry of the seven (Acts 6:6). But it is equally instructive—and also fascinating—to see what the leaders *didn't* do in response to the conflict as it is to observe what they did.

So let's take a closer look at what they didn't do. It's there in the latter part of Acts 6:2: "We apostles should [not] spend our time . . . running a food program." On the surface, this attitude doesn't seem very service oriented. In fact, just the opposite. But the leaders also made it clear where their time *should* be spent: in teaching the Word of God and in prayer (Acts 6:2, 4).

Here's the essence of the pastoral dilemma in most churches: How much time should the pastor devote to prayer and teaching and how much to other ministry? There's no question that pastors are tugged in multiple directions. As a consequence, they may be tempted to substitute *good* for the best. Sure, they can be involved in the food ministry. That's a good outreach for the church. But pastors can't be tugged in so many directions that they sacrifice spending time in prayer and in the Word of God.

Let's pray for pastors to have time in the Word. Let's pray for them to *make* time to be in the Word. And let's pray for ourselves as church members to find ways to take up the work of ministry so that our pastors will have time to be in the Word.

> Then we apostles can spend our time in prayer and teaching the word.
> ACTS 6:4

Reflection

Twenty pastors gathered at a retreat in the mountains of North Carolina. The purpose of the retreat, of course, was to get away and relax. Another primary purpose was to help the pastors get a clearer and healthier focus on their lives and ministries.

The leader of the retreat opened with these words: "Pastors, you have a piece of paper and a pen in front of you. You will note that the paper has this heading: *Neglect*. You will also note that there are five lines below the heading. I want you to take a few minutes and reflect on which aspects of your life you neglect the most because of other responsibilities and because of the expectations placed on you. In other words, where are you *not* spending sufficient time? You don't have to write them in order of priority, but I want you to write only five items."

The pastors quickly grabbed their pens and started writing. Though a few seemed to need some time to think about their responses, most wrote quickly and without hesitation. When the leader saw that everyone was done, he gathered the responses and began reviewing them silently.

The pastors noticed that the leader placed most of the responses into one pile. Only a few were placed in a second pile. Then the leader spoke.

"You probably noticed that I put your responses into two piles," he began. "The first group represents those of you who had identical answers. In other words, you noted exactly the same five areas. There are seventeen in that group.

"Did you get that? Within about three minutes, seventeen out of twenty pastors wrote down five identical neglected items. Of the other three, two matched the big group with four of your responses, and the other matched three."

You could tell that the pastors were surprised by the virtually unanimous results. Maybe each one thought his struggles were unique. But heads began to nod as the leader went through each of the five consensus areas. He read them in no particular order since all five were present for most of the pastors.

One area of neglect was exercise and physical well-being. Clearly, taking care of themselves was one of the first things to fall by the wayside.

The second area of neglect was a physical issue as well: not getting enough rest and sleep. Because the pastors had so much to do and so many expectations placed on them, they stayed up too late and got up too early. No wonder they were constantly tired.

The third area was one identified by all twenty respondents: They often neglected their families. As the retreat progressed, many cried as they told stories of hurting their wives and children.

By now, you may have guessed the final two areas of neglect: time in prayer and time in the Word. Most of the pastors said their time in the Bible was often limited to sermon preparation or teaching a lesson. They knew they needed to spend time in the Word both personally and devotionally, but they struggled to develop a consistent discipline.

We must pray for our pastors to create the time and make the commitment to read and study God's Word for their own refreshment and edification. It's the only way they can have an effective ministry.

Praying for My Pastor

Lord, send my pastor with hunger to your Word.

Remind him that, in Acts 2:42, the believers "devoted themselves to the apostles' teaching," which is the substance of the Bible we have today. May my pastor be consumed with reading your Word.

I pray that my pastor will devote adequate time in the Word each week to prepare his sermon.

I pray that my pastor will devote adequate time in the Word for every occasion where he does Bible teaching.

But I also pray that my pastor will devote abundant time in the

Word just for himself. Let him hear from you through your Word. Let him be empowered by you through your Word.

Remind the church that the pastor will only have time to be in the Bible if the members of the church are doing the work of ministry so he won't feel as if he must fill all the gaps.

I know my pastor believes your Word, Lord. May he live in your Word as well.

In Jesus' name,
Amen.

Counselor

A RECENT CONVERSATION with a pastor about counseling reminded me how challenging this issue can be.

The pastor was in his first church. He was seminary trained and very smart, and he carried himself well. His credentials and gravitas seemed well suited for counseling.

Until he had to counsel someone.

His first appointment was with a couple who had been married for about two years. The wife said over the phone that the marriage was struggling, but her husband was willing to come to counseling with her.

In preparation, the pastor reviewed some of the biblical texts on marriage. He had not taken a counseling course in college or seminary, but he had purchased a book that addressed key issues such as marriage counseling.

He was ready. Until they walked into his office.

Within five minutes, the husband and wife were screaming at

each other. The husband laced his tirade with some choice words of profanity, and his wife responded in kind.

The pastor did not even remember how the appointment ended. He hoped he remembered to pray with the couple.

Every week, pastors are asked to counsel people in their congregations. But most pastors have neither the training nor the desire to mediate disagreements and listen to a plethora of problems and challenges unless they are specifically spiritual or biblical questions. Though most pastors will refer serious counseling needs to others more suited for the task, they are still the first point of contact for many people seeking counseling help.

Considering the number of churches in the United States alone, pastors are counseling about a million people a week. It is a daunting task. It is often a fearful task.

We must pray for pastors who counsel others. We must pray they will have wisdom and discernment.

> Joyful is the person who finds wisdom,
>   the one who gains understanding.
> PROVERBS 3:13

Reflection

Clark was not looking forward to this counseling appointment. He wanted to help Preston, an eleven-year-old boy whose parents had recently divorced, but he had never counseled a child in similar circumstances and wasn't sure he knew what to say.

Clark was familiar with the family's struggles. Preston's father, Rick, had had an affair with a coworker. When the affair came to light, Rick had begged his wife, Jennifer, for forgiveness, and she decided to give him another chance. Though she struggled with feelings of betrayal, Jennifer wanted her marriage to work, and she wanted Preston to have his dad at home.

Despite the pain Rick had caused her, Jennifer had agreed to go with him to a professional marriage counselor. She hoped for a new beginning but sensed that something was still not right. She felt that her husband was only going through the motions.

She was right.

Within two months of the time that Jennifer forgave him for his infidelity, Rick resumed the affair with his coworker.

Now the marriage was over.

Jennifer continued to get counseling from a marriage and family therapist, and she knew that Preston needed help as well. After his dad moved out of the house, Preston was angry, confused, and grieving. The only person he was willing to talk to was Pastor Clark, whom he trusted and held in high esteem.

Clark could not tell Jennifer no. Preston really needed help. Clark hoped he could give the child some assurances and then refer him to someone more qualified. Jennifer agreed with the plan.

The pastor's heart broke when Preston came into his office. The boy was sad and broken. His dad had left home—abandoning his mom for a woman he didn't know. His grief was palpable.

After a few minutes of small talk, Clark asked with compassion, "Preston, how can I help you?"

With tears falling down his cheeks, the young boy looked at his pastor and said, "Pastor Clark, will you please tell my dad to come home?"

It happens every day. Pastors are confronted with pain. They are confronted with grief. They are confronted with anger.

Most people don't walk into a pastor's office wanting to know the latest perspectives on eschatology. They come with burdens and pain. They need help. By and large, pastors truly want to help. But most are not trained or qualified for a counseling ministry.

Your pastor will most likely be counseling someone this week. The situation may be simple, but it is likely a complex mess. Even when they refer people to someone else, pastors need wisdom and discernment for the moment.

Pray for your pastor as he counsels others.

Praying for My Pastor

God, I can't even imagine all the decisions my pastor has to make each week. I certainly can't imagine all the people who come to him for help, advice, and wisdom.

Please give my pastor insight. Let him receive your guidance and not be dependent on himself. Give him the right words to say to those he counsels. Give him the wisdom to point people in the right direction. Give him the discernment to know when he needs to bring others into the situation.

And, Lord, I pray for those whom he counsels. Many come with deep needs and open wounds. Many come seeking answers only you can provide. May your Spirit minister to them even as my pastor does as well.

Thank you, God, for being the great Counselor. You indeed know our hurts and needs before we know them ourselves. And thank you for looking after my pastor as he cares for others.

In Jesus' name,
Amen.

Caregiver

COUNSELING, in some ways, is a subset of pastoral care. Pastors who counsel will meet with one person or a few people concerning a specific need. Pastoral care, on the other hand, is broader. It includes counseling, hospital visits, home hospice visits, telephone calls, emails, and other forms of communication with those in need.

One pastor told me he devotes about ten hours a week to those serving in the military. Not only does he provide pastoral care at a nearby military base, but he also continues to care for the men and women as they are deployed around the world.

He marvels at the number of videoconferences he has been able to have with soldiers on deployment. Those soldiers have told the pastor he is a lifeline as they face both danger and loneliness.

Hospital visits can be one of the more time-consuming ministries for pastors. If the church is in a rural area or small town, church members may be hospitalized in the nearest city. One round trip might consume an entire day. If the church is in a more populated area, there may be several hospitals nearby, and the pastor must navigate city traffic to reach each one.

More important than all these issues, though, is the need of the moment. During hospital visits, pastors must sometimes comfort those who are fearful of an upcoming surgery or who are facing death.

I don't often hear pastors complain about the stress they feel with these visits, but the cumulative effect of the varied emotions can be challenging.

Pastors need wisdom for pastoral care. They need strength for pastoral care. They need our prayers for pastoral care.

> Guard yourselves and God's people. Feed and shepherd God's flock—his church, purchased with his own blood—over which the Holy Spirit has appointed you as leaders.
>
> ACTS 20:28

Reflection

Jason loved being a pastor. There weren't many aspects of his ministry he dreaded.

"I would say the main exceptions are committee and business meetings," he said with a laugh.

He was still at his first church, and he had been there for a decade. Unless God clearly called him away, Jason had no desire to move. He loved the idea of a lifetime ministry to one church.

Clearly, in the course of ten years, he had experienced a lot of ministry. He was no longer a rookie. Like other pastors, he had been with his members on the mountaintops and in the valleys of their celebrations and needs. In fact, he had just returned from the hospital, where he had celebrated with a couple who were welcoming a new child into the world. Mother and baby were both doing well.

Then the phone rang.

He had known the call would come one day—and probably soon. But even though Jason thought he had prepared himself for this moment, when the word came, he hung up the phone and wept.

The call was about his best friend, Max. Max and Jason had hit it off ten years ago when Jason first came to the church, and their friendship evolved into one of those rare bonds between a church member and his pastor. They were almost like brothers, the kind of friends who would die for one another.

Except now Max was the one who was about to die. He was only forty-two years old, but the aggressive cancer he'd been diagnosed with had spread rapidly.

Jason thought about Max's wife, Patsy, and their four precious children. How would they make it without the husband and dad they loved so deeply? Jason wondered how *he* would make it without Max.

Max had hoped he would make it to Christmas, but eight days ago he'd taken a turn for the worse and been hospitalized. Jason had been to see him every day. Now the word was that they were giving him less than two days to live. In truth, it could be at any moment.

Jason had made many pastoral care visits to the hospital. God had used him as a source of strength for many, including several who were dying. But now he was making what would likely be his last pastoral care visit to his best friend. He was going there to say goodbye.

Jason wanted to be strong for Max, but his friend knew him too well. He would not be able to hide his emotions from Max.

Jason walked slowly out to his car. As he got in, he thought, *This is the saddest trip I've ever made.*

Pastors make a variety of pastoral care calls. A few are for celebrations, but many are painful. We should pray for pastors to have compassion, wisdom, strength, and hope for these visits.

Pastoral care should not be done apart from God's strength. It is our role as church members to pray for that strength.

Praying for My Pastor

God, I can't imagine the breadth and depth of my pastor's ministry to others. The emotional swings must be challenging, if not daunting. He needs you.

Please give him your strength.

God, I can't imagine the questions he is asked every time he makes a pastoral care visit. He needs you.

Please give him your wisdom.

God, I can't imagine the pain he sees in the eyes of others. He must be challenged every single day to look beyond the pain to see you. He needs you.

Please give him your hope.

And when he returns home from a wearying day of pastoral care, give him an extra measure of your strength, wisdom, and hope to care for those closest to him, his own family. He really needs you.

In Jesus' name,

Amen.

Expectations

HAVE YOU EVER THOUGHT ABOUT all the expectations placed on a pastor?

If you haven't, you are not alone. Most church members have no idea. Here are a few examples.

Pastors are expected to preach. Okay, that's self-evident. But they are also expected to preach *well*. Good sermons take hours to prepare.

Pastors are expected to counsel people whenever the need arises. They are also expected to visit people in the hospital, at the nursing home, and sometimes at home.

Pastors are expected to lead the church and be good administrators. Church members often have widely divergent ideas on what good leadership looks like.

Pastors are expected to officiate weddings and funerals. Almost every pastor has a story of cutting short a vacation to do a funeral.

Pastors are expected to attend committee meetings, business meetings, missions meetings, and meetings to plan meetings.

Pastors are expected to have near-perfect families. This expectation is not articulated until something goes wrong.

Pastors are expected to be active in the community. Many church members have different ideas about this priority.

Pastors are expected to respond to phone calls, text messages, social media direct messages, and an occasional piece of snail mail. They are expected to respond promptly. One pastor shared that he was criticized for not responding to a church member who messaged him a new theological question on Facebook every day.

Pastors are on call 24/7 for emergencies. Most pastors don't have the luxury of sharing that load. They are always on call. Always.

The list is longer, much longer. This sample, however, should give you an idea of what is expected of pastors every day and every week. And it should give you a greater urgency to pray for your pastor.

I can do everything through Christ, who gives me strength.
PHILIPPIANS 4:13

Reflection

Lawrence tried hard. He really did.

For years, the forty-year-old pastor had done everything he could to respond promptly to church members. Sometimes it was an emergency, and he dropped everything to go to those in need. Sometimes the situation was not urgent, but he still tried to respond promptly.

But Lawrence was tired, very tired. He did not know whether he could continue at his current pace.

Maybe, he thought, *today will be a restful day.*

He was too optimistic.

It was a Friday. Lawrence tried to take Fridays off as much as possible to spend time with his wife. It was often his only day off each week.

The day did not begin well. Before 9:00 a.m., he got a call from the church treasurer.

"I think we need to have an emergency meeting," the treasurer said with total seriousness. "At our current spending pace, we will be out of cash in three months. I called two of our elders to meet at ten. You need to join us."

Lawrence went to the two-hour meeting. The two elders who had been called were astute businessmen. They looked at the treasurer's numbers and did not see the urgency. In fact, they saw some errors in his calculations. They concluded that the financial situation was really not that bad. Lawrence hardly said a word in the meeting. All he knew was that he had wasted two hours of his day.

As he was driving home, he got a call from the church assistant. A teenage church member had been in a serious automobile accident. He drove to the hospital to meet with the anxious parents.

After he'd been sitting with the parents for more than an hour, a physician came out and shared the extent of the young man's injuries. Some were pretty bad, but nothing was life-threatening. Lawrence called his wife, Marcia, and asked if they could go to a restaurant for lunch.

Lawrence and Marcia got through their meal without interruption. But as they were heading home, Marcia got a text.

"It's Brenda," she told Lawrence. "She and Chris had another big fight. She texted me because she didn't want to bother you. I think you need to go talk to Chris. He's packing his bags and threatening to leave."

Lawrence sighed. If Marcia had not insisted, he probably would not have gone to meet with Chris. This wasn't the first time the man had made this threat. Lawrence knew he couldn't fix Chris's anger problem.

By the time he talked some sense into Chris and headed home, it was late afternoon. When he walked into the house, he could tell Marcia was in a serious phone conversation.

"It's Coach Wells. He said Bryan broke his leg at basketball practice."

Lawrence and Marcia headed to the emergency room to be with their eldest child. It was a pretty nasty break. An orthopedic surgeon said he needed surgery right away. It ended up being a long night. Marcia stayed at the hospital with Bryan.

When Lawrence got home, he checked his phone. He had ignored it while he was at the hospital. There were four missed calls, a voicemail, and a text message—all from the same person. Lawrence had forgotten he was supposed to show up for a surprise fiftieth birthday party for a church member. He read the text, and his hand started shaking. It was from the wife of the birthday celebrant:

"Pastor, I heard Bryan broke his leg and had surgery. Sorry. But you made this commitment a long time ago. I can't believe you couldn't have gotten away for a few minutes. SMH."

"Yes," Lawrence sighed to himself. "I'm shaking my head too."

Praying for My Pastor

Lord, most of us have no idea how much is expected of our pastor.

We often act as if our pastor is omniscient and omnipresent. We expect him to know everything and to be everywhere.

First, I pray that you would give our pastor wisdom and discernment. Give him your priorities instead of his own or the priorities of the church members. Guide him when to say yes and when to say no. Make it clear that he should please only you, instead of needing to please others.

Next I pray, God, that you would remind him that his first line of ministry is his own family. May he never forget that those closest to him should receive ministry first. Give him the grace and strength to maintain this priority toward those he loves so deeply.

Finally, I pray, Lord, give our pastor rest. As he seeks to do your will and choose your paths and priorities, teach him to slow down and seek your restoration and strength.

Then, and only then, can he really be the pastor you have called him to be.

In Jesus' name,
Amen.

Weddings

"A PASTOR WHO DOES A WEDDING WELL is like a referee who calls a game well."

No, the analogy is not meant to communicate that weddings require a referee. The pastor who said those words meant that pastors need to be as much in the background as possible. If the pastor gets noticed in a wedding, it's usually not a good sign. The wedding should be centered on God and focused on the bride and the groom.

Some pastors do three or four weddings a year. Others do twenty or thirty. One pastor shared that he did forty weddings one year.

A wedding is a day of celebration. It is the pastor's role to make certain the wedding ceremony focuses on how God blesses and celebrates weddings. For many pastors, accepting an invitation to officiate a wedding has four stages.

First, he must decide whether he will do the wedding. It's

not always an easy decision. Many pastors will not marry non-Christians. Some will not perform the ceremony of a divorced person if they determine that the marriage ended for reasons other than those permitted by biblical doctrine. Whenever a pastor declines to officiate a wedding, someone inevitably is mad, hurt, or both. Usually both.

The second stage is premarital counseling. Some pastors do this counseling themselves. Others refer couples to trained counselors.

The third stage is the wedding rehearsal. This typically involves setting aside time for the rehearsal itself and a rehearsal dinner.

The wedding, of course, is the fourth and final stage. Many pastors use the same script for every ceremony unless the bride and groom request modifications. A reception or party usually follows the wedding.

As we pray for pastors who officiate weddings, let us pray that they will keep all aspects of the wedding God-centered. Emotions can run high during any of the stages. Pastors are expected to keep everything on an even keel and keep the focus on God.

"God made them male and female" from the beginning of creation. "This explains why a man leaves his father and mother and is joined to his wife, and the two are united into one." Since they are no longer two but one, let no one split apart what God has joined together.

MARK 10:6-9

Reflection

Kirk got the bad news on a Friday morning. He heard it directly from his son, Jacob.

"Dad, there's an electrical outage at the football stadium," Jacob said in a somber voice. "They can't fix the problem until tomorrow. The game has been moved to Saturday night."

Kirk sighed without responding.

"Look, Dad, I know you have a wedding to do Saturday night," Jacob said firmly. "It's really okay. You haven't missed a game the past two years. You can't back out of a wedding at the last minute."

Kirk knew his son was right, and he wasn't upset about doing the wedding. He was just sorry he would miss the game. Jacob was the starting quarterback for the high school team, and Kirk loved watching him play. Kirk himself had been a high school player, but he hadn't had Jacob's passing arm. Instead, he'd been a pretty good running back.

Kirk took seriously the solemnity and celebration of marriage. He prayed over each wedding. He prayed for both the bride and groom. He prayed that the couple would sincerely honor their vows "until death do us part."

Kirk had already declined the invitation to the rehearsal dinner because the game had originally been set for Friday night. The couple had even graciously agreed to move the rehearsal an hour earlier so Kirk could make it to the game.

"Well," Kirk mumbled to himself, "that was a nice gesture offered in vain."

The rehearsal went smoothly that night. As he always did, Kirk reminded everyone that the wedding was both a celebration and a worship service. And he reminded them that marriage is one of God's best gifts to humanity. Kirk always did a good job of keeping things in perspective in the marriage ceremony.

The next day, the wedding began right on time. Kirk chastised himself for being a bit down about missing the game. After all, God had called him for these moments. He should be thanking God for the honor of being allowed to lead such a holy ceremony.

The bride, Amy, had asked Kirk if he could get there thirty minutes early. She wanted to get the wedding photos with him done before the ceremony. The other photos could wait until after it was over. It was an unusual request, but the pastor had been happy to comply.

As with most of the weddings Kirk officiated, everything went off without a hitch. It was truly a God-centered celebration. There were tears of joy as the bride and groom said, "I do," and then led the recessional to conclude the service.

As always, the pastor waited until the last of the wedding party had departed before saying a prayer to dismiss the congregation. He was about to head to the reception when the father of the bride grabbed him by the arm. "I need you to come with me," he said. Kirk had no idea why, but he went along as requested.

The two men took a back route to the room where the wedding party was getting ready for photos. Amy walked right up to Kirk.

"Pastor," she said with a mischievous smile. "I know the sacrifice you made to be here. Your photos are done, and I don't want you coming to the reception. We are winning 7–0 at halftime. Jacob threw a touchdown pass. If you leave right now, you can make it for the second half."

Kirk stood speechless and was surprised to feel tears on his cheeks. Amy hugged him and told him again to leave.

"Dear God," Kirk prayed as he jogged to his car. "Thank you for this incredible wedding and this wonderful church. I am a man most blessed."

He found a place in the stands and caught his son's eye. Jacob grinned from ear to ear and waved to his dad. He passed for two more touchdowns.

They won 21–10.

Praying for My Pastor

Thank you, God, for a pastor who loves his flock. Thank you for the sacrifices he makes every week for us.

And thank you for his spiritual leadership in weddings and for how he reminds us of the holiness and celebration of the moment.

Give him wisdom as he offers premarital counseling or refers couples to someone else. Open the hearts and minds of the future brides and grooms as our wise pastor leads them to understand the future that lies before them.

Please guide our pastor at rehearsals as he not only provides direction but also sets a spiritual tone for the wedding ceremonies to follow.

And be with him as he officiates the services themselves. Thank you that he always reminds us of the importance and sanctity of marriage and for how he always points those attending to Christ.

And, yes, thank you for the sacrifices he has to make to do these weddings. Please bless his efforts.

In Jesus' name,

Amen.

Funerals

TYPICALLY, WE THINK ALL FUNERALS are basically the same. The deceased is remembered. Bible verses are read and prayers are said. Usually, the service includes some type of music. And someone may speak or give a eulogy.

Pretty straightforward, right? Not really. At least not from the pastor's perspective.

Though almost every pastor views funerals as an essential part of the ministry, they do tend to disrupt schedules. You'll rarely hear pastors complain about missing study time or a ballgame to conduct a funeral, but there is some angst when a funeral interrupts a pastor's vacation. One pastor was in Hawaii when he got word that the church matriarch had died.

The church, by the way, was in Maine. The vacation was cut short.

When an obvious and devoted Christian dies after a long, full life, the funeral can truly be a celebration. The good and faithful servant is welcomed home by the loving Father. But ask the pastor about the funeral of a five-year-old boy who drowned. Or the teenage girl who was killed by a drunk driver. Or the young dad who left behind a wife and three children under the age of ten. Those funerals are gut-wrenching.

Though many pastors have experience with difficult funerals, it doesn't remove the emotion of the moment. Experience can't take away the tears when the pastor sees little children who have lost a parent.

Perhaps the most difficult funeral is for someone who was not a Christian. How can a pastor who believes John 14:6—that no one comes to the Father except through Jesus—offer hope and compassion to the family of the deceased? Certainly, he can give a clear gospel presentation. But what can he say about the person's eternal home? Most pastors simply don't address that painful reality.

Do you see why your pastor needs prayer for funerals? Do you see how you should pray for your pastor in light of these challenges?

Pray for your pastor. Pray for your pastor when he does funerals.

> O death, where is your victory?
>   O death, where is your sting?
> 1 CORINTHIANS 15:55

Reflection

It was the largest funeral Mitt had ever officiated. No other time even came close. The church's worship center could accommodate six hundred people, but more than one thousand came.

Fortunately, the mild spring weather allowed for overflow outside, with screens that allowed everyone to see and hear the service.

The size of the crowd was not an issue for Mitt. The greater the number of people, the greater the opportunity to share the gospel.

But Mitt struggled with two issues. First, Jeremy had been only seventeen years old when he was shot and killed in a hunting accident. His youth and the fact that he was accidentally shot by his best friend made the moment intensely tragic. Everyone in town knew Jeremy. He was an all-state running back on the high school football team. He likely would have been the class valedictorian. The size of the crowd attested to his popularity.

But there was a second and even greater issue. Jeremy and his family had attended church, but Mitt did not have the assurance that Jeremy was Christian. In fact, he had counseled Jeremy just four months earlier. Despite Mitt's probing questions about faith, Jeremy did not seem to have given his life to Christ.

Mitt hoped that Jeremy had had a conversion experience since he'd last met with him. It was certainly possible. But he had his doubts. He felt he was about to do the funeral of a non-Christian, but one that most people would think was saved.

He had asked his wife to pray for him. He had asked a good friend to pray for him. And now, right before the funeral was set to begin, Mitt was praying for himself.

For this one funeral, Mitt had the opportunity to share the gospel of Christ with a large crowd. For this one funeral, Mitt had the opportunity to demonstrate Christ's compassion to the teenager who accidentally shot his best friend; to that teenager's family; and, of course, to Jeremy's family.

Yet, for this one funeral, he had to walk carefully and truthfully through the challenge that Jeremy was likely not a believer. Though he would never presume to say what was on his mind about Jeremy, it affected him and his message.

As he walked out to the church podium and viewed the packed crowd, Mitt swallowed hard. He saw the pain in the eyes of Jeremy's family and in the eyes of his best friend's family.

He felt the pain of his own uncertainty about Jeremy. He asked for God's wisdom and God's words for the moment.

This pastor truly needed prayer.

Praying for My Pastor

God, give my pastor the right words—wise and compassionate words—when he preaches at funerals.

For funerals of people whose death seems to make little sense, give him the heart to know how to comfort their families and provide hope.

For those funerals where someone has died suddenly and without warning, provide my pastor a clear measure of the Holy Spirit's presence and power.

For those funerals where the person who died was not a Christian, give my pastor a way to provide hope for those who are left behind. Help him articulate the gospel clearly. Give the family the hope their loved one did not have.

For all the funerals he leads, provide him an extra measure of your grace, God, so he can be a conduit of that grace to those who are grieving.

Above all, I pray, Lord, that my pastor will be a powerful ambassador of Jesus. In Christ and Christ alone are hope, comfort, promise, and victory found.

In Jesus' name,
Amen.

Weariness

IF YOU HAVE READ each of the designated days of prayer up to now, you know that your pastor has a lot of responsibilities. Not only is the work never ending, but many of the responsibilities are fraught with emotion. Counseling. Pastoral care. Hospital visits. Weddings. Funerals. You get the picture.

When pastors speak of the things that make them weary, they often mention one or two categories. The first is conflict in the church and the steady drip of criticism. Infighting and negativity are true energy sappers.

The second is simply the cumulative effect of the ups and downs of vocational ministry. A good example is this email from a pastor:

I'm tired. For a while I couldn't pinpoint the source of my weariness, so I went to my doctor. He couldn't find anything physically wrong with me, but he prescribed some antidepressants. I decided I didn't want to take them. Finally, I asked my wife why she thought I was so tired. I should have asked her first. She simply said, "It's everything."

I didn't understand at first, but then she explained. It made perfect sense. It's not any one thing; it's the roller coaster of emotions of ministry. We are celebrating a birth or a new birth at one moment in the day, then we are sitting at the bedside of a wonderful Christian who is about to enter heaven. It's not one thing. It's everything.

We should pray for our pastors to lean on Christ and his strength in all they do. All the time.

Jesus said, "Come to me, all of you who are weary and carry heavy burdens, and I will give you rest."
MATTHEW 11:28

Reflection

It was 5:00 a.m., and Pastor Jorge was already working on his sermon. Two funerals during the week had put him behind schedule. He would have to put in a few extra hours to complete the sermon. It wasn't like him to still be working on a sermon on Friday, but it had been a busier-than-usual week.

Or had it?

The more Jorge thought about this week compared to other weeks, the more he realized that it wasn't any busier, just different. The two funerals threw a good bit of his schedule off, but if it hadn't been that, it likely would have been something else. Busy was normal.

He tried to do most of his hospital visits on Fridays. Of course, he had to adjust when there was a serious need on another day of the week. Jorge realized how blessed he was to have Randy as an associate pastor. Randy was a bi-vocational pharmacist. Somehow, he was able to make hospital visits on the days when Jorge could not. And Jorge knew that Randy would call him if the need was serious.

Today, Jorge planned to make three hospital visits. Though it wasn't that many, these three would be especially challenging. Each patient was in a different hospital, and they were all thirty minutes apart. More if there was traffic, which there often was.

Jorge had a quick lunch and kissed his wife, Maria, at the door. He told her he hoped to be back in about three hours if everything went well.

Unfortunately, everything did not go well. Traffic was unusually heavy. Counting drive time, Jorge spent more than four hours visiting his members in the hospital.

Then, as he prepared to go home, he got a call from his assistant. There was a fire at the company owned by one of his elders. Jorge called Maria to give her the news. The company was an hour-plus drive away, but Jorge felt that he should be there for the elder.

The building had been badly damaged, but it was not totally destroyed. While Jorge sat with the elder, he overheard his conversation with the insurance agent. They found a temporary place for his company to relocate while repairs were made on the building.

On the drive home, Jorge took advantage of technology and returned several calls using his Bluetooth connection. One of the calls was incredibly encouraging. A couple who had struggled to have children let the pastor know the wife was pregnant. Another call was not as encouraging. Mary Lou, one of Jorge's persistent critics, complained that his sermons were still too long. "Last week's sermon was twenty-eight minutes!" she exclaimed.

The rest of the calls were routine, and he was able to get them done.

When he arrived home, Maria greeted him with a compassionate smile.

"I'm sorry, honey," she began, "Marge dropped off these papers and said you needed to sign them. They are for the refinancing of the church mortgage."

Jorge did not understand why the bank insisted on having his signature, but he complied. It took him more than an hour to skim through all the documents and sign them.

Finally, at 10:00 p.m., he could get to his emails. Forty-two unread messages awaited him. One was from Mary Lou, with "A Suggestion" on the subject line. Jorge cringed, but he decided to read that one first to get it out of the way.

"Pastor Jorge," the email began, "here is a link to a sermon by an incredible pastor. His text is the same one you preached on last week. I think he has some insights you missed. And his sermon is only twenty-four minutes long."

Maria poked her head into the study. "How are you doing, honey?" she asked with sincere empathy.

Jorge turned around, looked at his wife, and smiled.

"I'm tired. I am incredibly tired."

Praying for My Pastor

Lord, give my pastor rest. Give him sufficient hours to pause and to sleep, to refresh his mind and body.

But give him more, I pray. Provide for him not only physical rest but the true rest that comes from leaning on you, trusting you, and getting his strength from you.

When he forgets to pray for that strength, help us church members to rise up and pray on his behalf.

Give our pastor strength to celebrate with us when we see God at work.

Give our pastor strength to go through the day with the many activities to which he is called.

Give our pastor strength so he can pray and be in your Word without weariness.

Give our pastor strength to lead, shepherd, and equip this church. May he depend on you and you alone.

When the weariness seems too heavy, when the burdens seem too great, when the complaints become too vicious, and when the expectations are too many, teach him to turn to you. For you and you alone will strengthen him and give him rest.

In Jesus' name,
Amen.

Leading

MOST PASTORS, when they first enter the vocation, are surprised by how much leadership and administration it requires. Pastors are supposed to understand the budget. They need to know enough parliamentary procedure to lead meetings. They are required to lead both paid and volunteer staff. Many pastors have to deal with a plethora of organizational details when they have any type of facility additions or major repairs.

One pastor shared that he spent two days working with a lay leader to solicit, review, and accept bids for a new HVAC system. The list of administrative issues is unending.

Some pastors may enjoy this aspect of pastoral ministry. They may have come from the business world prior to entering the strange world of vocational ministry. Budgetary and administrative issues are second nature to them.

But most pastors do not have such a background. And most

pastors did not receive any training in this area prior to accepting their first pastorate. It makes sense, then, that the majority of pastors do not feel equipped in these matters, and more than a few detest administrative leadership.

So how do we pray for pastors facing administrative challenges, particularly those who do not feel particularly adept at this facet of pastoral ministry? First, we can pray for God's wisdom for them. They know they need that wisdom. They eagerly seek that wisdom.

Second, we can pray that these pastors will have other staff or church members who will walk with them or even do much of the administrative work for them. Others can come alongside these pastors and help them in areas that aren't their strengths.

Finally, we can pray that pastors will not become so burdened with administrative tasks that they forget their primary calling. They are to devote themselves to prayer and to the ministry of the Word (Acts 6:4).

> Select seven men who are well respected and are full
> of the Spirit and wisdom. We will give them this
> responsibility. Then we apostles can spend our time in
> prayer and teaching the word.
>
> ACTS 6:3-4

Reflection

Brad really did not care for this time of year. It had nothing to do with the season. It was all about the church budget.

Brad had been a pastor for eight years. He was well loved by most of the members of the church. Like most pastors, he'd been through a couple of rough years that seemed like a decade at the time, but he was well past that era. The past few years had been really positive. He loved being a pastor.

Well, most of the time.

Around October, the volunteer treasurer would drop off a budget worksheet. Brad was expected to fill in about seventy blanks, each one representing a budget decision for the next year.

The exercise was by no means simple, especially for Brad. For example, how did he know how much to put in the spot for employee health insurance? He often had to ask ten questions just to fill in one blank on the worksheet.

This process had begun with the previous pastor, who had come to the church from the business world and who thrived on such administrative tasks.

The church had become accustomed to having the pastor initiate the annual budget. When Brad arrived, they naturally assumed he would do the same.

Brad could feel a lump form in his throat when the worksheet hit his desk for the annual exercise. He knew he would be spending dozens of hours trying to get those silly blanks filled in. Even his wife had begun to dread the annual ritual. She could see a change in her husband's demeanor that lasted for more than a month. And the change was not good.

Caleb had observed the budgeting process the previous year. He was the general manager of one of the largest employers in town. His company had relocated his family nearly two years ago. Caleb not only observed the process; he observed his pastor. He could see Brad's visceral reaction to the annual budget. He could feel the tension when he walked into Brad's office to help with "a few of those dang blanks," to use Brad's words.

Caleb asked Brad a straightforward question: "Why do you lead the budget process each year? It's obvious you don't enjoy it."

Brad looked up. "I not only don't enjoy it, I'm also not good at it."

"Look, Brad, I hope you don't mind," Caleb said carefully, "but I went to the budget committee and shared my observations about the annual budget. I told them you only did it because the church seemed to expect it, not because you enjoyed it."

"What did they say?" Brad asked as he put down his pen and glasses.

"They told me it was fine for me to lead the process if you were okay with it," Caleb responded.

Then the unexpected happened.

Pastor Brad got up from his desk, put his arms around Caleb, and gave him a tremendous bear hug.

"I guess this means you're okay with giving it up," Caleb deadpanned.

Praying for My Pastor

God, help our church to understand that every pastor isn't good at everything; that every pastor can't do everything; and that every pastor doesn't want to do everything.

If my pastor loves administrative work, show him places where he can thrive.

If administration is not his gift or desire, raise up others around him who can take that role from him.

Lord, give my pastor peace when he has to say no, especially when he simply cannot or does not want to do certain tasks in the church.

Above all, God, give him space, time, and wisdom for the two most important ministries he was called to do: prayer and the teaching of your Word.

Give me and others the eyes to see places in the church where we can fill in the gaps.

Please, Lord, teach our church to be the body of Christ we were called to be.

In Jesus' name,

Amen.

Others

MOST PASTORS HAVE THREE ROLES as they work with others in the church.

One role is supervising full-time and part-time staff. Pastors are expected to oversee the work of the ministry and administrative staff of the church. In many normative churches, the staff might be limited to one or two part-timers.

A second role is that of subordinate. Pastors are often under the authority of an elder board or a denominational or network official. They are accountable to these groups or individuals in their work as pastors.

The third role is working with laypeople. A church is not healthy unless the members are doing most of the work of ministry. The pastor is called to both equip and work with the laity in his church. In this role, he is neither supervisor nor subordinate. He works alongside many church members to accomplish the work of ministry in the church.

Relationships are always tricky, and pastors must manage their relationships with others carefully. When any relationship with the pastor becomes strained, the entire church suffers. Most every pastor has a story of a fractured relationship in the church. The pastor is hurt. The other party is hurt. And the church is hurt.

We should pray regularly for unity in the church, but we should pray specifically for unity in the relationships the pastor has with others. One bad relationship is not only painful; it is harmful to the entire body of Christ: "If one part suffers, all the parts suffer with it" (1 Corinthians 12:26).

> Always be humble and gentle. Be patient with each other, making allowance for each other's faults because of your love. Make every effort to keep yourselves united in the Spirit, binding yourselves together with peace.
> EPHESIANS 4:2-3

Reflection

It was one of the greatest celebrations of Rod's ministry. But it became one of the saddest parts of his ministry.

Rod was the pastor of a growing church in Northern California. When the church reached five hundred in worship attendance, Rod saw the need for a second key leader on staff. The budget had grown sufficiently that the church was able to hire someone to fill an executive pastor role.

Even better, thought Rod, he knew the perfect person for the position. He knew that his friend Tom would fit the culture and work perfectly. He and Tom had met when they both served on staff at a large church. Rod had been the associate pastor of administration at that church, and Tom had been the associate pastor of pastoral care. As peers, they became fast friends.

Tom was not an unknown. Rod had worked with him closely. He knew his work ethic, his character, and his great family. He was excited to present the idea to the board.

Much to Rod's surprise, the board was very cautious about the decision. Rod saw the risk as minimal—in fact, much less risk than with any other candidate. He knew Tom very well. But the board was cautious because of their friendship.

"When you bring a friend onto your team and now he works for you," the chairman of the elders said, "the dynamics of your friendship change."

Rod continued to push, and the board relented. He couldn't wait to call his friend.

The first few weeks after Tom came on board went just as Rod expected. The two friends were having a great time.

Then it changed with one simple request.

Rod asked Tom to complete a specific ministry task within a reasonable deadline. But Tom not only failed to accomplish the task; he never even started it. He didn't like Rod telling him what to do.

Rod did not understand at first. He gave Tom another task and saw the same result. But it soon became clear, Tom saw Rod as a peer and a friend, not as his boss. Rod *was* the boss, but he didn't expect it to adversely affect his friendship.

The relationship deteriorated. Rod felt betrayed by Tom, whose insubordination was making Rod look bad. Tom felt betrayed by Rod, who was supposed to be his friend and look out for him. The strained relationship became evident to many in the church. And when the chairman of the elders made an appointment to meet with him, Rod knew exactly what the topic would be. The chairman wanted to talk about Tom.

Rod had to make a decision, but how could he let Tom go? He had moved him and his family cross-country from Virginia just seven months ago. What would happen to him now? What would happen to his family? The elders had cautioned Rod. How did he miss it?

Praying for My Pastor

Lord, keep my pastor strong and humble in the many relationships he has in the church.

Give him humility as he interacts with others of diverse perspectives and backgrounds. Give him an open mind and open heart to listen well and respond well.

Give him wisdom to lead well and to be led well.

Give him courage to make the right decisions, not necessarily the easiest or most popular decisions. And give him the assurance that the right decision remains the right decision even when some people respond negatively.

Remind him that his relationships with others in the church are a key factor in the unity of our congregation. Give him a willingness to yield when he needs to yield. Give him clarity and determination when he needs to stand firm.

I pray as well, God, for those who interact with him. May both parties have a spirit of humility and service. And may both parties be completely guided by, led by, and filled with your Holy Spirit.

In Jesus' name,
Amen.

Encouragement

HER NAME IS MARGARET.

Though I have changed other names in the book thus far, I decided not to change Margaret's. Why would I not allow her the anonymity afforded to others? To be honest, I hope Margaret sees this devotional. I want her to read about herself. I want her to know what a difference she has made.

Though I have not personalized most of this thirty-day challenge, my writing about Margaret is intensely personal. My three sons are all in vocational ministry, and two of them are pastors. One of them is Margaret's pastor. Let me tell you why I love her.

She is a constant encourager to my son and his family. She encourages him privately. She encourages him publicly. In fact, I can count on Margaret to say something on many of the posts by and about my son on social media.

Does she criticize my son for his work as a pastor? Frankly, no.

She realizes that any pastor has plenty of critics and a dearth of encouragers. She makes it a point to be an encourager. Fervently. Consistently.

When COVID-19 hit the world in 2020, Margaret started listening to the livestreamed services from another one of my sons. Though several hundred miles away, she has become an encourager for another Rainer pastor.

I thank God for this lady. I love how she loves my sons and their families.

And I pray for a lot more Margarets in our churches. There are plenty of critics but a paucity of consistent encouragers.

Thank you, Margaret. May your tribe increase.

> Encourage each other and build each other up, just as you are already doing.

I THESSALONIANS 5:11

Reflection

The rumblings in the church did not bode well for the business meeting. Pastor Michael had already received significant criticism about the decision to adopt a dying church. Many of the church's members were not familiar with the idea of a multisite church. As one curmudgeon said, "We don't need a second building to look after, clear across town."

Michael was taken aback by the criticism. The church they were adopting was four miles away, in a neighborhood with hundreds of unreached families. The facilities were still in decent shape, and the church had no debt. But the congregation was dwindling away; only twelve members remained.

"What is going on?" Michael muttered to himself. "We are saving a church from death, and we have a great opportunity to reach a lot of people."

Uh-oh, Michael thought as he walked into the fellowship hall. The room was full for the business meeting. It was a bad sign when this many people showed up. Most members skipped the business meetings unless a fight was about to break out.

Michael tried to feign a smile as he spoke to different church members. But he could feel the tension in the room. He wondered if the motion to adopt the church would even pass.

Then Lillian walked into the room.

To know Lillian was to love her. She cringed when people called her the church matriarch because it implied she was a power broker who wanted to control the church. But Lillian was a servant, not a seeker of power. She encouraged; she did not criticize.

In fact, Lillian was one of those encouragers who not only spoke positively about other people but also had their back when others spoke negatively.

The moment Lillian walked into the room, heads turned to see the senior saint smiling from ear to ear. Michael should have known right then he had nothing to fear.

The meeting began with general business, but everyone was waiting for the big issue, the adoption of the other church. When the moderator announced the next item on the agenda, the room fell quiet. The tension was palpable.

Then Lillian spoke.

"Mr. Moderator," she said clearly and with enthusiasm. "I would like to move we adopt this wonderful church. And after we have a second to the motion, I would like to speak to it."

The second was made, and Lillian proceeded with what she wanted to say. She spoke about the incredible opportunity the current church would have to reach a new neighborhood. She spoke about how wonderful it was that the other church would not have to close. She said the area would still have a gospel witness.

She paused for a moment before speaking with deep emotion about Pastor Michael. She pointed to his heartfelt desire to spread the gospel. She mentioned his leadership and courage in leading the church to make such a move.

Lillian closed with these simple words: "Aren't we blessed to have Pastor Michael lead and serve our church?"

It was over before it was over. There was no heated discussion. Just a few more praises, and the vote was taken. Unanimous. Maybe a few didn't vote, but no one spoke in opposition.

Lillian the encourager had done it again.

Praying for My Pastor

God, teach me to be an encourager in my church.

There are plenty of critics, so raise up more encouragers in our church. Help them see how they could make a huge difference in our congregation. And as the church makes a difference, help them see that the Kingdom is influenced for good.

Remind me each day not only to pray for my pastor and the church staff but to encourage them as well. May I not grow weary in this ministry but become more emboldened every day.

Lord, help my pastor to be encouraged. He needs it. He faces not only critics but spiritual warfare every day. Encourage not only him but his family, as well. Let them know they are loved by you and that they are loved by us church members as well.

I am thankful, God, for the gift of my pastor. May I never take him for granted. Instead, may I demonstrate love and encouragement every day.

In Jesus' name,

Amen.

Courage

LEADERSHIP BOTHERS SOME CHURCH MEMBERS.

Let me clarify. Some church members are bothered by thinking of their pastor as a leader.

Pastors are supposed to be servants. Pastors are called to be preachers. Pastors are called to be teachers. Pastors are supposed to be shepherds and caregivers.

But some think that pastors are not supposed to be leaders. And they don't realize that some leadership decisions require courage.

The aversion to this topic is easy to understand, even if you disagree. Church members often see leadership as a secular role. It is something of importance in the corporate world. Or the sports world. Or the political world.

From this perspective, then, courageous leadership is seen as a trait that doesn't fit with pastoral ministry.

Of course, courageous leadership is an important topic in the

Bible. Jesus led his disciples with courage. Paul led several churches with courage. Moses had to be taught courageous leadership principles by his father-in-law, Jethro.

I have worked with numerous pastors who struggled because they didn't grasp the importance of leadership. Or perhaps they didn't think they were leaders, so they avoided leading. They preached well. They taught well. They did pastoral care well. But they felt woefully inadequate when they were confronted with decisions that required courageous leadership.

As we've seen, pastors have to make leadership decisions every day, almost without exception. Some of those decisions are routine; others require courage.

Most pastors feel as if they are well prepared for preaching, biblical teaching, and the activities commonly associated with pastoral care. But they bemoan their lack of preparation for dealing with leadership decisions that require courage.

Pastors need our prayers as leaders. Pastors need wisdom to lead. Pastors need God's wisdom to lead. Pastors need courage for many of their decisions.

Such should be our prayer.

This is my command—be strong and courageous! Do not be afraid or discouraged. For the LORD your God is with you wherever you go.

JOSHUA 1:9

Reflection

It was the worst day Patrick could ever remember as a pastor.

Stated simply, the church where he served was on the verge

of a split. He did not see any way apart from God's miraculous intervention that it could be avoided.

Patrick was in his fourth year at the church. The search committee that had originally called him hadn't told him about the power group that operated in the congregation. This group included seven to ten people, depending on how you counted. But their influence was much wider. Of the 250 active members, about 80 would follow the lead of this toxic group.

Patrick understood the dynamics well. Though one-third of the congregation was tied to the power group, an equal number were ready for change. They were tired of the bullies and particularly their leader, Don, who manipulated the congregation to get his way. Don regularly reminded people in the church that he and his sycophants "paid the bills."

Finally, the group that was ready for change took steps to remove the power group members from places of authority and replace them with members who would serve the church biblically and graciously.

Don could sense the tide turning against him and his group. He knew the pastor would be the deciding factor in this tragic struggle. Patrick's influence would tip the balance.

Patrick was greatly perplexed. He knew what was at stake. "They never taught me this at seminary," he said.

On the one hand, he wished those opposing the power group would be willing to wait a little longer for the situation to resolve itself naturally. Like Don, most members of the power group were elderly and might soon retire from their positions of influence without having to be removed by the congregation.

Patrick wanted to avoid conflict if possible, but he no longer had the option of waiting. The concerned group clearly felt that Don and his cronies had been strong-arming the church long enough.

Both sides waited for Patrick to weigh in. Patrick himself considered the consequences. Though he did not have access to the giving records, the church financial assistant told him that those most closely associated with the power group contributed 40 percent of the budget. They did indeed pay the bills.

Patrick called an older pastor who was an informal mentor of his. He gave him the pertinent information. The more seasoned pastor listened carefully and then asked a simple question.

"Patrick, what is the right thing to do?"

The answer was obvious. Patrick knew it was time to confront the ugly behavior of the power group. He knew who was wrong and who was right. He had been so blinded by the potential consequences that he'd failed to ask the basic question.

Patrick understood what was about to happen. He knew the church was about to take a major hit. But he also knew the right decision.

It was time.

It was time for courage.

He prayed that God would be with him and the church.

Then he picked up the phone and called Don.

Praying for My Pastor

Lord, I have prayed for wisdom for my pastor, but this time I pray for him to have courage as he faces the issues and decisions that come up every week.

First, I pray for him to have clarity. Help him see the decisions he has to make and the consequences of those decisions through your eyes.

Second, I pray for him to be a peacemaker. Often, courage requires him to make decisions that will make people unhappy. As much as possible, give him the wisdom and clarity to be a shepherd to those who are not pleased with him. Teach him to love them anyway.

Finally, give him the courage to make the right decision. Not necessarily the easiest decision. Not necessarily the most popular decision. But the right decision.

And when his courageous decisions result in pain for him and others, remind him that you are with him even in the valley of such difficult moments.

God, please give my pastor courage.
In Jesus' name,
Amen.

Hope

THE ROOM WAS FILLED WITH PASTORS. The question the speaker asked elicited the expected answers: "What is a nonnegotiable characteristic a pastor must have?"

"Believes and preaches the Word."

"Loves his family."

"Loves the people in the church."

"Is committed to his call."

Then a voice from the back spoke with authority: "Must communicate hope."

There was a pause in the room. It was as if the pastors had not given that characteristic much thought, but they couldn't disagree with it. In fact, it became the driving topic for the next thirty minutes. How best can a pastor communicate hope?

The pastors were in agreement that hope was ultimately found in the person of Jesus Christ, but there was a sense of uncertainty about how that hope was communicated day by day. While the preaching ministry was the primary venue to communicate the hope of the gospel, there was less clarity on how to make it practical in the everyday lives of church members.

One pastor reflected on the days after COVID-19 hit the world. Back then, he told the group, his church members were looking for hope. He had focused on how to communicate that message in such a vulnerable time. But it also became clear that he had to focus on the message of hope in other times as well, beyond the pandemic.

Then one pastor articulated a question that seemed to be the elephant in the room: "How do *pastors* find hope?" It was not a theological question as much as it was a cry for help. There were obviously some hurting pastors present.

It was a good question. How many church members pray for their pastors, that these servants of God would find hope day by day?

> I pray that God, the source of hope, will fill you
> completely with joy and peace because you trust in him.
> Then you will overflow with confident hope through the
> power of the Holy Spirit.
> ROMANS 15:13

Reflection

They could not delay the decision any longer.

Kyle and his wife, Molly, were sitting at the kitchen table confronted with a challenging decision. Kyle had been approached by another church more than five hundred miles away. It was, in some ways, his dream church. The congregation seemed to be a perfect fit for him and his family.

Still, Kyle and Molly loved their present church. They had been there eight years. Their two children, now middle school age, had practically grown up in the church. Kyle and Molly knew it would be a tough adjustment for them, but they knew their kids would ultimately do fine.

Kyle was less objective about the potential move than Molly was. Sure, the new church was bigger, much bigger. And that likely meant they wouldn't have to live paycheck to paycheck as they did now. But Kyle reminded Molly that he would also have three other pastors on staff. That would give him time he did not currently have. In that sense, it would be a great move for their family.

Molly did not want to be negative about the potential move. She knew her husband was excited. She did not want to dampen his enthusiasm. She had been praying that God would give them clarity. That's all she wanted: to be in the will of God. She didn't necessarily want a larger church, a larger paycheck, or a larger staff. She wanted the will of God.

"Kyle," she began cautiously. "I can see there are clear advantages to moving. You are right on so many counts. But let's think about this a little more. We know what the advantages are, but we don't know any of the downsides. There is no such thing as a perfect church. Can you call some pastors in the area to see what they say?"

Molly continued the conversation with the same caution. "Let me ask you this," she said. "What are the reasons to leave our church? I always believed the call of God had a push and a pull. We can see the pull as reasons to go to the next church.

But what are the reasons to push away from where we are right now? Don't we need a call *away* from a church as much as a call *to* a church?"

Kyle listened to his wife attentively. She was wise, and he knew she could offer perspectives he did not have.

He thought for a moment and said, "I guess one big reason we might be pushed to leave is the apathy in the church here. I feel it more than ever. It's like we don't have the hope we once had."

Molly nodded and said, "I don't mean to start an argument, but aren't you supposed to be the leader? If the church doesn't have hope, could it be that it's because you don't have hope?"

The couple got silent.

Two days later, Kyle called the prospective church. He told them God had not released him from his church. He was staying.

Praying for My Pastor

Lord, I state the obvious in this prayer, but I want you to know that I know my pastor is human.

He struggles at times. He can get discouraged. He is not always full of hope.

I guess, Lord, I'm saying I need patience for those times when my pastor is less than perfect. I have to admit that I want him to be upbeat all the time. I want him to be happy all the time. I want him to be a conveyor of hope all the time.

I can sense it in our church. When our pastor is not hopeful, we are not hopeful. I know it shouldn't be that way. Our hope should be in Christ and Christ alone. But the pastor is our leader. We are affected by his demeanor and posture.

So, God, I am praying that you would instill your hope in him so that he might lead us with hope.

And may we be reminded again and again to pray for our pastor to be encouraged and to have hope.

It really does make a difference.

In Jesus' name,

Amen.

Loss

PASTORS DEAL WITH LOSS on a regular basis.

I get it. Everyone deals with loss, and many people deal with deep and painful losses.

But consider for a moment the unique nature of the losses that pastors experience. First, they deal with the death of friends and family. While everyone experiences that pain at some point in their lives, pastors are confronted with it multiple times a year. They deal frequently with deaths, funerals, and grief.

Don't think for a minute that pastors are unaffected by these losses. Yes, pastors become somewhat accustomed to conducting funerals, but they are inevitably touched by the grief they see in others. That grief is often compounded when the death is unexpected or if the death is of a young person.

Pastors feel the loss of friends, as well. When they were in college or seminary, they typically had a great support group and an abundance of friends. Many who become pastors after working in the secular world have a similar network of friends.

But pastors often have no true friends in their churches. It's tough to be both a friend and a pastor to church members. And once they leave the workplace or seminary, the network they once had is no longer in place. Pastors feel the loss of friends. Many are lonely.

Pastors feel an acute loss when members decide to leave the church, especially if they are not moving out of town. It is not unusual for departing members to be the people in whom the pastor has invested the most time.

Indeed, I have heard more than one pastor say that losing church members is an intensely painful loss because it feels like a betrayal.

Pastors feel the pain of losses. We must pray for them regularly.

> The LORD is close to the brokenhearted;
>> he rescues those whose spirits are crushed.

PSALM 34:18

Reflection

The pastor could see it coming. Unfortunately, in his twenty-two years of pastoral ministry, he had seen it too many times.

Arthur knew why Ivan and Melanie had made an appointment to see him. They were planning to leave the church.

The couple fit the classic pattern of departing church members. First, they had become intensely involved in multiple ministries. They were probably spending too much time doing church ministry. When Arthur kindly suggested to Ivan and Melanie that they should be careful about doing so much, Melanie had responded with a satisfied smile, "You can't burn out doing the Lord's work."

The next stage is aloofness. The couple had become less friendly to Arthur. Indeed, they tried not to make eye contact or speak to him unless absolutely necessary. Arthur made repeated attempts to greet them and engage with them but, usually, to no avail. He also called them a couple of times to check on them. Their responses were always evasive.

Next comes the stage of waning commitment. Sometimes, the manifestation of this stage is poor execution of ministry commitments, including no-shows. At other times, it comes as resignation from ministries and programs. For Ivan and Melanie, the pattern was to quietly fade away from active involvement.

The final stage is departure—which is often, but not always, communicated. Arthur was certain he was ten minutes away from hearing about the couple's departure. He anticipated they would tell him they were not pleased with a program or a priority. They might also add that they "weren't being fed." The latter trope was particularly painful.

Arthur had been through this process many times in his pastoral ministry, and it never got easier. When he talked with other pastors, he heard similar responses and expressions of emotions. It was indeed a painful loss.

Typically, the pastors had invested a lot of time with the members who ended up leaving, giving them multiple opportunities to do the ministries where they expressed interest and excitement.

When Ivan and Melanie arrived, Arthur tried to be cheerful and friendly, but he was already hurting before they said a word.

After some small talk, Melanie got to the point. "Pastor Arthur," she said with a smile. Arthur could have been wrong, but her smile seemed insincere. "We appreciate so much all you have done for us at the church. When we were new here, you gave us immediate opportunities for ministry. You really encouraged us to serve the Lord."

Arthur was waiting for the dagger, the perfunctory "We love you, but . . ."

Melanie continued, "But we don't think the church's middle-school program is best for our son, Doug. We volunteered to work in that ministry, and we could see clearly how it is lacking. With Doug about to enter middle school, we have to think about what is best for him."

Arthur drew a quiet breath and waited for the formal proclamation.

"So we are leaving the church. We plan to find a place that has a really good student ministry," Melanie said a bit too smugly.

Arthur was always tempted to remind departing members that their role was to serve, not to be served, and that role wouldn't change with a change of venue. But that biblical truth was never effective by the time people had arrived at their conclusion. He wondered how they would fare in another country that did not have the amenities of a Western church. But he remained silent and simply nodded.

Melanie seemed to be seeking some type of reaction from the pastor, so she decided to toss one more verbal salvo: "Honestly, Pastor Arthur, we really haven't been getting fed by your sermons."

Praying for My Pastor

No one knows the pain of loss better than you, Father.

You gave your one and only Son to die for us. You let him become sin so he could take the punishment for our sin. When I think of John 3:16, I am overwhelmed by your love and sacrifice.

Yes, God, you know the pain of loss.

My pastor has not faced losses that compare with yours, but he does know the pain of rejection, death, loneliness, and discouragement. Will you give him an extra measure of grace and comfort during these times of loss?

Be with him when he grieves the death of a church member. He is there for the funeral and to comfort the family. He has seen some of the most agonizing situations. He feels the pain. He feels the loss.

Be with him when he feels lonely perhaps because he may have no true friends. He had them before he went into vocational ministry. But he does not have them now, at least those he sees regularly. He feels the loss of friendship.

Be with him when church members leave for silly and selfish reasons. He feels the pain personally. He often takes their decision personally. It is yet another loss for him.

My prayer for my pastor, Lord, is for your presence to be known powerfully during these times of loss.

Let him know that you are sufficient in all things, including these times of loss.

In Jesus' name,
Amen.

Failure

HOW DO YOU DEFINE SUCCESS in vocational ministry?

On the surface, it might seem simple. Success in ministry is being faithful to God. Okay, but what does that look like?

Many pastors can't tell you what success looks like, but they seem to know how to define failure. Indeed, many pastors probably see themselves more as failures than as successes. Let's look at a few examples.

There is the pastor that worked with a couple for months to try to save their marriage. He even got the church to help with the cost of a marriage counselor. The couple ended up getting divorced. The pastor feels like a failure.

There is the pastor whose church has about seventy-five people in average worship attendance. In the course of a year, only two people have become followers of Christ through the church's ministry, and those two were personally evangelized by the pastor. In other words, the entire church membership reached no one for Christ in a year. The pastor feels like a failure.

There is the pastor whose church saw a 25 percent reduction in its annual giving. They had to let go the only other paid staff member, a part-time worship leader. The pastor feels like a failure.

Do you get the picture? The examples are endless. Pastors rarely feel that they succeed at anything. But they sure know when they have failed. And if they don't feel like a failure already, they will likely hear from a church member where they are falling short.

> My health may fail, and my spirit may grow weak,
> but God remains the strength of my heart;
> he is mine forever.

PSALM 73:26

Reflection

"I've hit a wall."

Roger was not the first person to make that comment, but his fatigue and discouragement were no less real.

The metaphor refers to some type of blockage. In Roger's case, it was struggling to write his sermons each week. And he was not alone. Tens of thousands of pastors struggle every week. It's not an unusual occurrence.

Those who don't understand the dynamics of sermon preparation may think that pastors develop their sermons with ease—like it's second nature. Think about it, though. Most pastors prepare about fifty different sermons a year. Every single week, they seek God's hand to study, think, craft, and write a message.

Yes, God is with these pastors. But they still hit roadblocks at times. They still stare at the biblical text and a blank computer screen. They can feel the stress.

Roger had been preaching expository sermons for several years, working his way through entire books of the Bible or major parts of a book. Because of this, he didn't need to decide which Bible text to preach from each week. He simply started with chapter 1, verse 1 and continued the series through the end of the book.

Though choosing the biblical text certainly helps, there is much more that must be done to prepare a good sermon. Expository preaching deals with the text in its historical context. A good sermon captures the attention of the congregation. A good sermon has real application for the people listening. And not every verse or section of Scripture lends itself to easy explication. No wonder pastors feel as if they've hit a wall on occasion.

This particular week, Roger could not remember a time when he had been this frustrated in sermon preparation. While he typically took ten to fifteen hours to prepare his weekly sermons, he was already at twenty hours with much work yet to be done.

Like every pastor, Roger didn't have the luxury of taking a break and skipping the sermon because of his frustration. He had to push through.

Much to his own surprise, when he finally got it done, he felt good about the finished sermon. He felt that God had truly been with him. He was now looking forward to preaching it on Sunday morning.

Though Roger was a bit weary that Sunday, he was sufficiently excited about the message to keep his energy up. But when he went into his office to pray with the elders before the worship service, the newest and youngest elder made a poor attempt at humor: "Hey, Pastor, it must be nice to work only one hour a week."

Roger had lost count of how many times he had heard that line. But every church member who had said it over the years acted like it was an original thought. This time, however, it stung a bit more. Perhaps it was because the new elder trotted out the well-worn joke in front of all the others. Or perhaps it was because Roger had struggled so much this week.

He tried to shake off his annoyance as he walked to the pulpit to preach. Considering the challenges of the week, he felt pretty good by the time the twenty-eight-minute message was over.

He greeted several members as they left the service. There was not an abundance of compliments, but he knew better than to judge by silence.

Then Ruby came up to him. Roger noticed she had been waiting until most of the others had left. She spoke quickly and firmly: "Pastor, I just feel led by God to tell you this. Your sermons are not connecting. I really think you are cutting your preparation time short. We need to be better fed."

Roger could not remember the rest of the brief conversation. He was hurt. He kept thinking to himself, as he walked dejectedly to his car, *I guess I really am a failure.*

Praying for My Pastor

God, give my pastor the assurance that he is not a failure.

Please remind him again and again that he should only seek to please you. Gently nudge him when his primary goal is to please others. He will never please everyone in our church.

Point him to where he is a success in your eyes. Show him repeatedly the people whose lives have been changed under his ministry. Show him the new Christians, the marriages restored, and the men and women who have grown in their faith.

Lord, please give him an eternal perspective. You see things and changes that he may not always see. The short term can be discouraging and painful. The reward of being a good and faithful servant should be his goal.

And please lift up many church members to encourage him in such a way that he measures success in new ways. Point us church members to offer genuine compliments and encouragement so we can be reminders that he is a success in your eyes.

In Jesus' name,
Amen.

Anger

EVERY PASTOR GETS ANGRY AT TIMES.

Some pastors respond viscerally with an edge. That's not good.

Some pastors internalize their anger. That's not good either.

It's really tough for pastors to find the right balance.

You might wonder whether pastors should get angry at all. Simply stated, it's unfair to expect them not to have emotions, even emotions of anger. And until you've spent a season walking in their shoes, you will have no idea how pastors are often provoked.

In a recent social media survey at Church Answers, we heard about some really strange criticism that pastors receive. Here's a sample:

- "You didn't send me a thank-you note for my thank-you note."
- "I will leave the church if you don't put tissue seat covers in the restroom."

- "I would be happy to take your wife to the store to help her select some appropriate clothes."
- "You don't tell enough jokes when you preach."
- "I don't like the color of your beard."
- "Just because it's in the Bible doesn't mean you have to talk about it."
- "Your pregnant wife is faking morning sickness."

Yes, that is just a sample. Pastors can't help but get angry at some of the barbs thrown their way. The issue is not whether they get angry. It's more about what they do with their anger—holding on to it, lashing out, or responding in a godly way.

Before the day is over, your pastor will likely have to deal with a negative comment, email, social media post, or phone call. And he may get angry.

We don't need to pray that our pastors won't get angry. We need to pray that they'll respond well in their anger. It's a challenge. But they can do it in God's power.

A gentle answer deflects anger,
    but harsh words make tempers flare.
PROVERBS 15:1

Reflection

I wish the following story weren't true, but it is. Like every one of the examples used in this book, this event really happened. I've changed some of the details and names to protect churches and people, but the essence of everything in this book is factual.

The reason for this caveat is the possibility you won't believe the following story. It seems too strange and cruel to be true. But it really happened.

The church was in the Deep South. It was basically deacon-run. This means the deacons did not perform the biblical duties of a deacon. They weren't servants. They were a power cabal that ran the church.

Pastor Nathaniel knew something was up when he was asked to come to a meeting. He knew the church had a history of changing pastors every three years. He'd heard the stories about how the deacons would call a meeting and then the pastor would be gone. He had a sense this could be one of those meetings.

When he walked into the room, five deacons, all over the age of seventy, were waiting for him. The church had six deacons, but one was very elderly and infirm.

There was no small talk. The meeting was orchestrated to allow each of the five men to present a list of grievances—complaints that supposedly came from recent discussions with church members.

"Pastor, I have a complaint that you used church funds to buy a personal desk for yourself," the first deacon said with sickening false sincerity. Nathaniel had no access to church funds. The desk in question was in the church office, not his. The church treasurer had purchased the desk when the previous one collapsed.

The second deacon spoke up: "We have records that you used more vacation days than the two weeks you are allowed."

Nathaniel could feel his face turning red. Every one of the deacons knew he had taken three days to drive a 1,400-mile round-trip to perform his father's funeral. His father had died after Nathaniel's family had already taken their vacation, but the deacons knew he was allowed three personal days for emergencies.

But it was the third deacon's remarks that really irked him.

"Pastor," the deacon began smugly, "we have reports that your wife was seen alone with Carl, our worship leader."

That did it. All the accusations to this point had been fabrications based on some factual incident. But this third claim was totally false. And it slandered his godly wife.

Nathaniel felt his anger rising and prayed for self-control. But it was tough. He decided he was not going to wait to hear any more lies.

"I can see where this charade is going," he told the group with a surprisingly calm voice. "Just like you've done with every previous pastor, you will continue to dredge up false accusations until you get your way. Your goal is to get rid of me. You do this every three years, when you start to feel that the pastor is growing in favor with the members."

Nathaniel swallowed hard. He was ready to get this over with.

"Okay," he continued. "What are your terms? What type of severance are you offering if I leave quietly?"

The informal leader of the cabal replied, "Three months."

"Give me four months and I'm gone," Nathaniel said.

"Done," the deacon responded.

The temptation to blast the deacons was great, but Nathaniel simply walked out of the room. He prayed that God would help him control his anger as he drove home to tell his family and begin preparations for moving.

The deacons congratulated themselves and got down to the business of calling a new pastor.

Praying for My Pastor

Lord, help my pastor deal with his anger when he is confronted with unfair accusations and innuendo. Help him with his anger when he hears yet another criticism.

Any leader must deal with tough issues, but pastors seem to face them almost every day. Some pastors are short fused; others have a bit more self-control. But all pastors experience anger. It goes with the job description, unfortunately.

I know it's tough at times for my pastor to do the ministry he's called to do because he has so many distractions and complaints that could make him angry.

So, God, I pray for self-control for my pastor. I pray that he will know when to speak and when to be silent. At times, he will need to bite his tongue. At other times, he will need to respond appropriately and biblically.

I pray, above all, that his words, whether in anger or calm, would bring glory to you.

In Jesus' name,
Amen.

Temptation

MORAL FAILURES OF PASTORS have become common news. In fact, they've become so common that the news of a failure doesn't surprise us nearly as much as it did in the past.

Though these failures have been around as long as there has been temptation, they caught the attention of the general public with the televangelist scandals of the early 1980s. They were big news then. Not so much today.

Though it does us little good to rehash the issues of the past, they do serve as a good reminder. Pastors are human. Pastors are subject to temptation. Some pastors yield to it.

Do you remember 1 Peter 5:8? "Stay alert! Watch out for your great enemy, the devil. He prowls around like a roaring lion, looking for someone to devour." The devil doesn't want our churches to be a powerful gospel presence in our communities. He knows that if he can get to the pastors, he can do great damage to churches.

Your pastor is a clear and present danger to the devil. The enemy wants to take him down. He looks for every opportunity he can find to attack your pastor. He wants your pastor to yield to temptation.

Sometimes, the loneliness a pastor experiences can lead to sexual temptation. Sometimes, the financial pressures in a pastor's life can lead to financial temptation. But the devil works on a pastor's ego, as well. If a pastor thinks congregational adulation is true and deserved, he may yield to the temptation of power and control. It is a very dangerous situation when pastors begin to think they are invincible.

A pastor is in spiritual warfare every day. Though we could judge the many pastors who have fallen morally and publicly, we ought to be doing everything we can to protect our pastors from temptation.

Yes, we should have accountability measures for pastors. Yes, we should have policies in place that prevent opportunities for temptation. But even more, we should engage in the battle of spiritual warfare so that our pastors can, in God's power, succeed in their battles with the enemy.

Stated simply, we must pray for pastors that they will neither be put in places of temptation nor yield to temptation.

> Keep watch and pray, so that you will not give in to temptation. For the spirit is willing, but the body is weak!
> MATTHEW 26:41

Reflection

It's a scenario that has become all too common. A pastor admits to an affair with a church member. When confronted, he immediately confesses and resigns from the church.

The pastor now has an urgent mission before him. He must do everything he can to save his marriage and his family. At this point, he isn't sure whether his wife can move forward with the marriage since he has broken his vow.

The leaders in the church meet to discuss a number of sad agenda items. They must find someone, either internally or externally, to preach next week—and for the foreseeable future. They must decide what type of severance they will give the pastor. Some will argue that the pastor doesn't deserve a severance check, but others will insist that they must think of the family. It was the pastor's sin, but it affects his wife and three children as well. They settle on a compromise of three months' pay.

The leaders must also decide how to communicate the matter to the congregation. They decide to be as transparent as possible without giving the sordid details. The families of the two people who had the affair are victims as well and deserve some discretion.

A good bit of discussion centers on the steps to take with the church member involved in the relationship. The issue of her involvement cannot be ignored.

Thinking they have addressed all the key issues, the leaders are ready to end their meeting when the eldest elder speaks up. He is a quiet and gentle man and the epitome of wisdom.

"Folks," he says softly, "we are not finished. We have to address another issue. What is the church's role in this failure? I don't want to suggest that the pastor is not culpable; I just want us to realize where we might have failed as well."

He continues, "It is my understanding that the relationship began when the pastor counseled the young woman several times in privacy. No one could see them behind closed doors. We have mentioned in the past putting windows in the pastor's office, but we never did. We also don't have a formal policy in place. Should we look at that as well?"

The elderly gentleman surprises everyone in the room when they see tears on his cheeks. "Above all," he asks, "have we prayed for protection for our pastor? Have we been diligently engaging in the battle of spiritual warfare and asking God to protect him from temptation?"

He pauses before concluding, "I'm not suggesting at all that our pastor is not at fault. I'm simply asking whether the church did all we could. Did we really pray for our pastor?"

Praying for My Pastor

God, I can hear those words so clearly. I have memorized the verses. They are part of who I am.

In Matthew 6:9-13, you taught us to pray when you taught your disciples to pray. We call it the Lord's Prayer today.

> *Our Father in heaven,*
> *may your name be kept holy.*
> *May your Kingdom come soon.*
> *May your will be done on earth,*
> *as it is in heaven.*
> *Give us today the food we need,*
> *and forgive us our sins,*
> *as we have forgiven those who sin against us.*
> *And don't let us yield to temptation,*
> *but rescue us from the evil one.*

It is right there. It is a vital part of the prayer you taught us to pray. You taught us to pray not to enter temptation lest we lose the battle to the enemy.

Lord, remind me to pray that prayer not only for myself but for my pastor, as well.

Remind me of his humanity and his vulnerability. Remind me to pray for him today and every day.

Please protect my pastor from temptation.

In Jesus' name,

Amen.

Comparisons

COMPARISONS OF PASTORS have been around since we've had pastors. Paul writes about it in 1 Corinthians 1:12: "Some of you are saying, 'I am a follower of Paul.' Others are saying, 'I follow Apollos,' or 'I follow Peter,' or 'I follow only Christ.'"

In the first part of the twentieth century, local church pastors were compared to well-known radio preachers. In the latter part of the twentieth century, they were compared to television preachers. Now in the twenty-first century, the comparisons are to podcast preachers.

Church members can have idealized perceptions of pastors they don't know. These platform personalities often have charisma and extraordinary communication skills. It can be tempting to assume that their other pastoral gifts and abilities are extraordinary as well.

On the other hand, we see our own pastors up close and personal. We see their gifts, but we also see their foibles. We see them when they lose patience. We see them when they stumble in their sermons. We see their family members who, like the rest of us, are not perfect. And we often criticize them in their imperfections.

But those platform personalities will not be with you in your deepest valleys. They will not sit with you and comfort you when your loved one dies. They will not be there for weddings, funerals, celebrations, and moments of deep pain.

Your own pastor cares for you. The podcast pastor doesn't know you exist. Your own pastor is there for you. The podcast pastor is . . . well, on his podcast. Your own pastor loves you and prays for you. Podcast pastors can't pray for you by name because they don't know your name.

It is time to stop comparing apples and oranges.

It is time to be less critical and more prayerful.

It is time to be less judgmental and more forgiving.

It is time to be less expecting and more serving.

It is time to start some fresh patterns and habits.

May some of those habits include loving your pastor uncon-ditionally, evaluating your pastor graciously, and praying for your pastor more fervently.

I have not stopped thanking God for you. I pray for you constantly, asking God, the glorious Father of our Lord Jesus Christ, to give you spiritual wisdom and insight so that you might grow in your knowledge of God.
EPHESIANS 1:16-17

Reflection

Kirk thought it was unusual that the Groves family had missed three consecutive Sundays. The church was small enough to be able to see who was present and who was not in a given worship service. The Groveses made it easy. Their family of five always sat on the fourth row to Kirk's left. There were six in the family, but the oldest child was now in college.

Kirk had been pastor of Mt. Pleasant Community Church for eleven years. Growth had been slow but steady. He'd had opportunities to go to other churches, but he never felt released from his present assignment. Even more, he loved the church members deeply. Any thought of leaving them brought him pain.

When he called Jim Groves the next morning, the call went to voicemail. Again, that was not typical for Jim. He usually answered immediately when he saw the call was from his pastor. Kirk left a message, asking Jim to call him back.

In another out-of-character response, Jim waited for more than a day to return the call. When he did, Kirk could tell he was not himself. He seemed nervous, edgy. It took only a minute for Kirk to learn why.

The Groves family was visiting Pointe Church. It was the largest church in town. Mt. Pleasant had lost a few families to Pointe Church over the years, but most of the transfers had happened when the current pastor arrived three years earlier.

"Please don't take it personally, Pastor," Jim began.

Kirk sighed and braced himself for whatever Jim was about to say.

"We just feel like we are getting fed at Pointe Church," Jim said nervously. "You are a good preacher, but . . ."

He didn't finish the sentence. He didn't have to.

Four months later, Kirk's phone awakened him at 3:15 a.m. He looked at the caller ID. It was Jim Groves. His voice was nervous, but not like the previous call. Something was wrong.

"Pastor," Jim began, "Blake is in the hospital in critical condition." Blake was their oldest child, the one in college. "He's had a drug overdose. I . . . I didn't even know he was using drugs. We are on our way to the university hospital. I'm sorry to bother you, but could you meet us there? We really haven't gotten to know the pastor at Pointe Church. We don't know if Blake is going to make it."

After that last sentence, Jim began to sob. Kirk told him he would be there as soon as he could. He told his wife what was happening. She got up and began to pray for Blake. And she also prayed for her husband.

Kirk had a three-hour drive ahead of him. Counting the round trip, he spent nine hours on this pastoral call. He sat with the family until they got definitive news that Blake would survive.

Praying for My Pastor

Lord, remind our pastor that you love him just as he is.

When he is compared to other pastors in town, pastors on television, and pastors on podcasts, he must wonder at times whether he is adequate for this ministry to which you've called him.

Let my pastor know he is to be faithful to you and you alone. You will determine his level of success by the measure of his obedience to you. Church members cannot determine his worth in comparison to others.

God, give my pastor patience when he hears how wonderful another pastor is. Teach him to rejoice in the ministry of others, even when church members are, in essence, telling him he does not measure up.

And let us church members be very careful in making comparisons. We may know for certain that our own pastor is not perfect, but we must also know for certain that other pastors are not perfect either.

Give our pastor, Lord, the joy of his salvation and the celebration of his call, not only to ministry in general but to our church specifically.

In Jesus' name,
Amen.

Joy

IF YOU SPEND TIME ON SOCIAL MEDIA, you may have seen the meme. The before-and-after photos are an attempt at humor, but there is a sad irony to them.

The first photo shows a pastor at the beginning of his ministry at his first church. He is well dressed and smiling broadly, and his countenance is obviously one of joy.

The second photo shows the same pastor three years later. His clothes are disheveled, he looks as if he doesn't take care of himself, and his expression conveys a mixture of pain, grief, and anger. Certainly not joy.

The meme is an exaggeration, of course, but there is a truth to it as well. Many pastors enter their first pastorate with a combination of enthusiasm and idealism— which lasts until their first business meeting or the first critical remark offered right before they take the pulpit to preach.

Pastors will be the first ones to tell you we should have joy regardless of the circumstances. Joy doesn't depend on whether life is going our way or not. Joy is found in Christ and Christ alone. Joy is not a giddy happiness as much as it is a settled peace.

Your pastor believes that truth. Your pastor tries to embody that truth. But like anyone who experiences life's valleys, he doesn't always find it easy to *live* that truth every single day.

That's why we must pray for our pastors.

Pray they have joy. Every single day.

Always be full of joy in the Lord. I say it again—rejoice!
PHILIPPIANS 4:4

Reflection

Like most pastors, Jerome began at his first church with an abundance of enthusiasm. He was in his final year of seminary, and he anticipated putting his studies to practical use right from the outset. The seven members of the small church had seen these pastors come and go for decades.

By almost any standard, the church was old. The youngest member was sixty-eight. The oldest was ninety-one. Of the remaining five, two were in their seventies and three were in their eighties. The median age was eighty-five. They had been around the block in church life. So when Jerome exerted his spiritual gift of naiveté, they were quick to correct him and bring him back to reality. And when Jerome tried to lead toward some small changes, they offered stiff and successful resistance. In fact, the members were able to predict what Jerome would try to do with an uncanny degree of accuracy.

It didn't take long for the young pastor to become discouraged and disillusioned. Such was the path of almost every new pastor who came to the church. And every new pastor moved on after about two years. That wasn't the plan, but it was almost always the outcome.

After worship services one Sunday, Merle, the church patriarch, approached the pastor. He told Jerome the church had one home-bound member and she would welcome a pastoral visit. Jerome knew this was not a suggestion but a mandate. So he obliged and went to see Miss Opal that very afternoon. He assumed his role was to encourage her and pray for her. Little did he know he would be the encouraged one, not the encourager.

Miss Opal was probably close to ninety, but Jerome dared not ask. She had been in a wheelchair since she was a teenager. That's all she said; she offered no details.

Jerome had noticed that Miss Opal's home was on the more down-and-out side of town. He mentioned to her that her door was unlocked and ajar and that he feared for her safety.

The elderly lady responded with a howl of a laugh.

"Honey, I've been robbed more times than I can remember. Finally, I made it clear that anyone can come in at any time and take anything they want. They got the message. So they steal from me legally!"

Again she laughed heartily.

Jerome asked whether she was afraid of getting hurt, and she laughed again. "Look, Pastor, I'm already paralyzed from the waist down. They can't hurt me much more."

He tried another angle: "But when people steal from you, do you have anything for yourself? Do you have any food?"

There was that laugh again. Boisterous. Mischievous. Joyous.

"Honey," she said, "do I look like I'm starving? You see, people not only steal from me. They leave me stuff. They leave me food. I am never without. I am one blessed woman."

Jerome had planned to pray for Miss Opal, but she prayed for him instead. She prayed a prayer that was as genuine as he had ever heard. It was a prayer of joy. Pure joy.

When Jerome left, he placed his hand on the steering wheel and prayed before driving away, "Lord, forgive me. Forgive me when I have pity parties. Forgive me when I think I am in need. Forgive me for not having joy always."

After a pause, he concluded, "Make me more like Miss Opal, Lord, because she is the closest I have ever seen to a person who has Jesus shining through her."

As the pastor drove away, he found he was indeed joyous.

Praying for My Pastor

Lord, give my pastor joy.

Better yet, remind him of the joy he already has in you.

When he confronts tough times, I pray he will count it all joy.

When he has times of celebration, I pray he will count it all joy.

When he hears criticism, I pray he will count it all joy.

When he sees lives changed to be more like you, I pray he will count it all joy.

May the words of James 1:2-4 be his focus:

"Dear brothers and sisters, when troubles of any kind come your way, consider it an opportunity for great joy. For you know that when your faith is tested, your endurance has a chance to grow. So

let it grow, for when your endurance is fully developed, you will be perfect and complete, needing nothing."

Simply put, Lord, teach my pastor to rejoice at all times.

And teach us church members to pray for constant and abiding joy in his life.

In Jesus' name,

Amen.

Clarity

MANY ASPECTS OF PASTORAL MINISTRY are clear and unambiguous. For example, pastors are to preach the Word of God. Such is the task of most pastors every week.

Pastors are to pray; they lead their churches in prayer. The priority of both teaching the Word and leading in prayer is clear in Acts 6:4.

Pastors are to lead in evangelism by doing evangelism. This mandate is clear in Paul's words to Timothy: "Work at telling others the Good News, and fully carry out the ministry God has given you" (2 Timothy 4:5).

For a list of right priorities, we can look at the first church, the church in Jerusalem, where the main emphases were on teaching, fellowship, prayer, worship, generosity, and evangelism (Acts 2:42-47).

Most pastors are clear about the *what* of ministry. Where they need more clarity is knowing *how* to lead in these areas.

How does a pastor exhort and motivate the congregation to become evangelistic?

How does a pastor know how to lead with financial resources? Should more funds be expended for personnel? For facilities? For programs and ministries?

How does a pastor know how to reach the community where the church is located? How does the pastor encourage and motivate the church to be a gospel presence in the community?

As you pray for your pastor today, pray for the *how*.

Ears to hear and eyes to see—
    both are gifts from the LORD.
PROVERBS 20:12

Reflection

The evangelism committee meeting was one that Les really enjoyed. The pastor was not a fan of meetings in general, but this group of seven men and women was among his favorites.

Les thought for a moment about why he liked these meetings so much. He came up with two reasons right off the bat. First, they were positive people. He could not recall hearing a negative word or criticism from any member of the committee. Second, their enthusiasm was contagious. He was grateful to have such high-energy people on the evangelism committee. He hated to think what this committee would be like with a few curmudgeons on it.

But the challenge each year was the same. The pastor and the seven committee members wanted the church to become more evangelistic. They really wanted to reach more people with the gospel.

"Perhaps," one committee member noted, "we need to stop calling ourselves a *committee*. There is a sense in this church that the evangelism committee is like the finance committee. They take care of all the money, and we do all the evangelism. Maybe our name is hindering our efforts. The church may think that evangelism is the responsibility of only seven people."

To their credit, the evangelism committee did a good job of keeping evangelism before the church. In the past year, the emphasis was Invite Your One, which encouraged every member to invite someone to a worship service on a designated Sunday. The idea behind the emphasis was not so much a high attendance day as it was to create a culture of invitation. The more that members invited others to church, the more likely they would be to have a relationship with those people.

Pastor Les knew that relationships were key. In the past year, the church had celebrated fourteen new Christians, all of whom had become followers of Christ through a relationship with a church member. And all fourteen were active in the church today.

Les thought for a moment before sharing what was on his mind: "Folks, first we need to celebrate what God has done. We should not take lightly that over a dozen people have given their lives to Christ this year. I have no doubt that the work of this committee helped inspire our members to develop relationships and share the gospel. I thank God that he has used you in this way."

The pastor paused to look at each member of the committee, and then he continued, "But let me be transparent with you. We have about three hundred active members in our church—that is, those who are here at least twice a month. If we reached fourteen people with the gospel last year, it means it takes about twenty of our members to reach one person each year. We should celebrate the fourteen—*of course*. But why can't we, in God's power, reach one hundred with the gospel each year? With three hundred active members, such a goal seems reasonable."

The committee members all nodded.

"My challenge," Les continued, "is to have clarity on how to lead this church more faithfully in evangelism. I really need prayers for clarity."

He knew these seven men and women understood. He concluded with "I know the *what*. We are supposed to share the gospel. But I don't know the *how*. How do we get more of our members involved in reaching our community?"

The pastor spoke his last sentence with conviction: "Please pray for me to have clarity."

Praying for My Pastor

Lord, I rarely think about praying for my pastor to have clarity, but I pray for it now. He must make daily decisions with clarity. But he also must lead our church with a clear vision and strategy.

He can't have that clarity in his own power. I pray for you to give him clarity.

God, I have read in the Bible many times about Jesus healing the blind. Those miracles were true physical miracles. They were signs pointing to the Son of God.

Yet, Lord, you also have the power to give sight to those who need clarity. There will be times when our pastor does not have the precise vision to know where to lead us. But you can perform the miracle of sight and give him a clear vision.

I am so grateful for my pastor, Lord. I am grateful for how he loves us and leads us.

Give him your love to love us unconditionally, and give him your vision to lead us clearly.

In Jesus' name,

Amen.

Friends

EVERYONE NEEDS FRIENDS. We make friends in our neighborhoods, in our organizations, and in our workplaces.

Perhaps some of your best friends were your classmates in high school or college. Maybe you joined a local organization and found good friends. Or you may have some good friendships at work.

Pastors, on the other hand, often have difficulty finding good friends. Many pastors devote sixty or more hours a week to their churches, and they simply don't have the margin or time to devote to other places to find friends.

Some pastors find good friends in the church they serve, but they are the exceptions. More pastors are careful about getting too close to someone in the church. We all need friends in whom we can confide, but it usually isn't best to talk with someone in the church about problems in the church.

Even fewer pastors find close friends on the church staff. There is the obvious and possibly awkward situation where friends have a boss/subordinate relationship.

If you were to ask several pastors where they connected to their closest friends, one of the more common responses would be *college* or *seminary*. Indeed, it is a blessing to have such long-term friendships. With technology, it is easier than ever to stay connected with these friends, even if the geographical distance is great.

Still, it's not the same as having a friend in close proximity, someone you can call to meet for a cup of coffee or a meal.

Friendships are gifts. Pastors need good friends. We should pray for them to find local and loyal friends they can enjoy and in whom they can confide.

Two people are better off than one, for they can help each other succeed.

ECCLESIASTES 4:9

Reflection

Gary and Mack live in the same Southern town, with a population of about thirty thousand.

They are pastors in the same town, and both have been at their respective churches for eight years.

The similarities don't end there. The two men are a year apart in age, and both have three children of similar ages. They pastor similar size churches, and though Gary is a Baptist and Mack a Presbyterian, their congregations have much in common.

Here is a surprising bit of information about the two men: They didn't meet until they had been at their respective churches for seven years. In fact, they'd never heard of each other until a year ago.

Each man had decided to join a mentoring group that was mostly online. However, the group met in person once a year. When new members introduced themselves, Gary and Mack were shocked to discover they were from the same town.

Over the past year, the two men have become close friends. Almost every week, they will meet at one of their three favorite coffee shops—one more thing they found they had in common.

They consider their friendship a great gift. Though neither pastor is a golfer, they both love college football. They pull for different teams, but they love to talk football. But the most frequent conversation they have is about church life, specifically their own churches.

Gary and Mack are careful not to break confidences or use members' names in their conversations, but they do share stories. Both pastors love stories that have a funny or lighter note, but they are also transparent about serious matters, including their own struggles. Mack said he felt like a poor pastor because of his struggles. At least until Gary shared his own struggles.

Both men deal with power groups in their churches. They talk and pray about those situations on a regular basis.

Mack sums it up well: "I don't how I served as pastor before I met Gary. His friendship has been one of the best gifts I've ever received. Every pastor needs a good friend in town. Every pastor needs his own pastor."

Praying for My Pastor

God, please give my pastor a friend. Not just any friend but a good friend.

Give him the type of friend he can trust, in whom he can confide, and with whom he can laugh.

Let that friend be an encourager and counselor. And let my pastor reciprocate by encouraging and counseling.

When my pastor needs someone to whom he can turn—whether he is celebrating, grieving, laughing, or hurting—may that friend understand. May he listen without passing judgment. And may he pray for my pastor as well.

May that friend, Lord, be someone with whom my pastor can be himself. Pastors find themselves on guard and careful with their words, especially with us church members. I understand. One misconstrued sentence by a pastor can cause unintentional hurt.

And as my pastor draws strength through this friendship, may his friend draw strength as well.

Friends are incredible gifts.

I ask for that gift for my pastor, God.

In Jesus' name,

Amen.

Equipping

THE APOSTLE PAUL makes it clear in Ephesians 4:11-12: Pastors and teachers are to equip others to do ministry. That is how we build up the church, the body of Christ.

Most church members will affirm that pastors are equippers. But many church members do not realize that the role of equipping means that pastors cannot do a lot of the other ministry in the church. Somehow, pastors are expected not only to equip others but also to do most of the ministry themselves. In other words, the unbiblical assumption is that pastors are hired hands to do ministry for the church.

However, as we've seen in earlier chapters, the leaders of the first church in Jerusalem asserted and protected the priority of prayer, teaching the Word, and equipping the church. They said, "We apostles should spend our time teaching the word of God, not running a food program" (Acts 6:2).

Did you get that? The apostles said they should *not* be doing the

WHEN THE PEOPLE PRAY

ministry of giving food to the widows. Think how that response would go over in many churches today.

Instead, as they equipped others to feed the widows (Acts 6:5), the apostles were freed up to pray and teach the Word. They were freed up to equip others to do ministry.

The results are noted in Acts 6:7: "God's message continued to spread. The number of believers greatly increased in Jerusalem, and many of the Jewish priests were converted, too."

Pray for pastors to be able to equip others. The very health of the church is at stake.

These are the gifts Christ gave to the church: the apostles, the prophets, the evangelists, and the pastors and teachers. Their responsibility is to equip God's people to do his work and build up the church, the body of Christ.

EPHESIANS 4:11-12

Reflection

Gary and Mack, the two pastor friends introduced in yesterday's devotion, were meeting one summer day at one of their favorite coffee shops. They had their usual beverages of choice: black coffee for Gary and a vanilla latte for Mack.

"I am on the edge of burnout," Gary confided to his friend. "Sometimes, I think it's the nature of Baptist churches. The members see their pastor as an employee who works for them. Anytime a ministry needs to be done, they expect the pastor to do it. I know I'm supposed to be equipping others to do ministry, but I keep running into a brick wall."

"Look, Gary," Mack responded. "The problem is not limited

to Baptist churches. We Presbyterians have our own challenges. I do think, however, that churches with congregational polity have unique challenges. Because congregational churches seem to vote on almost everything, the members think they are the bosses. Believe me, I know. Baptists who have joined our Presbyterian church have been some of my biggest challenges."

Gary knew that Mack was not debating church polity. He was simply stating the reality of many churches.

"Here's my conundrum," Gary said after listening to his friend. "I know the problems. But I have not found the solutions."

Gary paused and took a sip of his coffee.

"My first problem is the one you stated," Gary continued. "Many of our members expect the pastor to be the hired hand to do ministry. With about three hundred active members, I am constantly responding to their requests, sometimes their demands. I wish I could take the time to teach them to do the ministry, but I don't have the time myself."

Gary saw his friend's wry smile.

"Look, dude," he said with mock disgust, "I know I should take the time to equip them. But I first have to teach and convince them that they need to be equipped. Some of them think their financial gifts are the dues they pay to be served by me. Frankly, I don't know where to begin."

Mack understood all too well. "You might have an additional challenge as well," he said. "Speaking for myself, sometimes I think, deep inside, I don't *want* to let go of ministry. Some of it is my ego. I want to prove my worth to the church. And if I stopped doing the ministries they think I should do, they would value me less. So the problem for me is twofold. The members expect me to do most of the ministry, and I'm afraid of letting it go lest my value be diminished in their eyes."

Mack took a long sip of his latte and concluded, "Maybe my problem is that I find my value in what others think of me instead of in Christ and Christ alone."

Praying for My Pastor

Lord, help my pastor to let go.

Give him both the wisdom and the strength to know when to let go. Remind him again and again that he is not to do all the work of ministry.

God, show my pastor how to become a better equipper of others. Give him the insight to find the time to make equipping a priority. Give him the courage to say no when he should.

I pray, Lord, for us church members. May we come forward more eagerly and expectantly to do ministry in our church. May we volunteer before we are asked. May our attitude be one of serving instead of being served.

Protect my pastor from burnout. First, let him be a leader who is willing to let go of tasks and ministries. Help him to understand that he can't hold on to so much. Burnout will be inevitable.

And show my pastor that his value is in Christ. It is not in his abilities, in his time, or in meeting the needs and requests of all the church members.

Lord, help my pastor to let go, and help us members to fill the gaps with joy and expectancy.

In Jesus' name,
Amen.

Love

IF YOU WERE TO ASK a typical church member where the Bible speaks of love, many would point to the words of Jesus. One example is a simple command he gives in John 15:17: "This is my command: Love each other."

Among Jesus' final words to his disciples was this admonition to love one another. He said that one of the marks of a true Christian is how he or she loves other people. Christ's words in John 13:34-35 are both powerful and relevant for today: "Now I am giving you a new commandment: Love each other. Just as I have loved you, you should love each other. Your love for one another will prove to the world that you are my disciples."

Ask any pastor about his greatest desire for his church, and he will reply with something similar to these two characteristics: *love* and *unity*. Those two traits are really two sides of the same coin. If you love one another, you will be unified. And if you seek unity, you will do so by demonstrating love.

Pastors understand that we cannot be an effective witness to the world unless we demonstrate love to one another within the church. That is the picture painted in Acts 2:46-47: "They worshiped together at the Temple each day, met in homes for the Lord's Supper, and shared their meals with great joy and generosity—all the while praising God and enjoying the goodwill of all the people. And each day the Lord added to their fellowship those who were being saved."

The reference to "all the people" is to those on the outside looking in. The church was a light of love and unity that drew many people to be saved.

Your pastor would rejoice if you prayed for love and unity in the church.

He would also welcome your prayers that the members show love not only to one another but to him, as well.

> Three things will last forever—faith, hope, and love—and the greatest of these is love.
>
> 1 CORINTHIANS 13:13

Reflection

It was a terrible month for Dale in many ways. He had just returned home after preaching the funeral of both his mom and his dad. His elderly parents had been passengers in a car hit by a drunk driver. All four people in the car were killed.

Dale had thought he was prepared for the deaths of his parents. They'd had some health struggles. In fact, they were on their way to the doctor when tragedy struck. Still, the suddenness of the accident and the death of both parents at the same time sent a shock through his system for which he was not prepared.

Undoubtedly, Dale was frail already. His adult son, Michael, had recently come to him and his wife, Lydia, to tell them he had a drug problem. He was admitting himself to a rehab center. Michael stood before the church the following Sunday and shared about his addiction and asked for prayers. The church responded with an outpouring of love and support.

When Dale and Lydia saw the grace and mercy poured out by the church members, they both wept openly in the worship service.

And now this tragedy. Michael had barely checked in at the rehab center when the news about Dale's parents came.

Dale told Lydia he was not sure he could continue as a pastor. He loved the church dearly. Though it was far from perfect, his nine years there had overall been very positive. But he was emotionally spent. How could he serve others when he was running on empty himself?

Lydia understood. She gave her husband two wise pieces of advice. First: Don't make a decision when you are so low emotionally. Second: Before quitting, consider taking some time off instead.

The two were in their family room discussing that very topic when they heard a sound—faint at first but growing in intensity. It was like the sound of angels, but it was people singing. It grew louder and louder. Lydia recognized the hymn first: "It Is Well."

When they walked outside to the front porch, they were blown away. Cars were parked as far as the eye could see and there were people everywhere.

And then there were the signs.

"We love you, Pastor and Lydia."

"We are praying for you."

"Jesus is with you."

"Your church loves you."

There were so many signs, so many people, and so much love.

And they were singing a capella. These were the words Dale and Lydia heard when they walked out to the porch:

When peace, like a river, attendeth my way,
When sorrows like sea billows roll;
Whatever my lot, thou hast taught me to say,
It is well, it is well with my soul.

Dale and Lydia wept openly and gratefully.

Before them was love, the love of Christ.

It was indeed well with their souls.

Praying for My Pastor

Dear Lord, above all the prayers I have for my church, please let the answer to this prayer be made clear and evident in our congregation. May we love one another.

May we put others before ourselves. May we see the joy of serving rather than being served.

May not only our actions reflect our love but may our words do so as well. Let us be encouragers and bearers of hope.

I pray fervently, God, that the church will become such an anomaly of love that the community will look on us with favor. Many will see the love of Jesus in us and be drawn to the Savior.

And please, Lord, show our pastor your love. Day after day with the heavy responsibilities of serving as pastor, would you lift him up, strengthen him, and sustain him with your love?

And teach us church members to love our pastor and his family as never before.

May this revival of love help us to discover more clearly the heart of the Father, the power of the Holy Spirit, and the sacrificial love of Jesus our Savior.

In Jesus' name,
Amen.

APPENDIX 1

Praying for My Pastor 30-Day Challenge

Key Idea

The purpose of this ministry is to have a specific thirty-day period of prayer for your pastor. This ministry can be initiated by the pastor, a staff member, or members of the congregation. Indeed, pastors should initiate this ministry without hesitation or reservation. The pastor who asks for prayer is acknowledging in humility that he needs prayer and would welcome church members praying for him.

Key Actions

- Plan this initiative at least three to five weeks in advance.
- Designate a leader to coordinate this short-term ministry.
- Use as many communication venues as possible to get members involved.

- Get members to commit to this ministry by signing up for it.
- Though it is always exciting to get many members participating, don't be discouraged if only a few sign up. There is power in the prayers of a few.
- Get a copy of *When the People Pray* for each participant. Get a few extras for latecomers.
- Explain the process: Simply read each of the thirty daily readings in the book and pray. It should take only about fifteen or twenty minutes a day.
- If possible, record three video testimonies and share them during your worship services. The first video will be a testimony of a church member sharing why he or she decided to participate in the ministry. The second and third videos should be shown at the midpoint and conclusion of the ministry, respectively. These videos will include a church member sharing how this ministry affected him or her.
- Give participants the opportunity to send a short note to the pastor during the thirty days. Though not required, this would be a source of great encouragement.
- Repeat this ministry focus with your church every year, if possible. Your church may want to conduct the ministry in October, which is pastor appreciation month. It is effective, however, anytime during the year.

Pastor's Intercessory Prayer Ministry

Key Idea

You've had an opportunity to develop a habit of praying for your pastor during the thirty days of this devotional. The Pastor's Intercessory Prayer Ministry will help you extend your prayer initiative into a longer, more sustained ministry.

This ministry is basic but profound. Church members commit to pray for the pastor for at least three to five minutes every day. Even if just a few people commit to this ongoing ministry, the power of prayer can have a profound and positive impact on both your pastor and the church. Many church members who have participated in praying for their pastor have stories of how their own lives were affected positively.

Key Actions

- Designate a leader to coordinate this short-term ministry.

- Use as many communication venues as possible to get members involved.
- Get members to commit to this ministry by signing up for it.
- Plan an initial meeting—either in person or by videoconference—with those who have committed.
- Emphasize that the participants should not miss a day of prayer but that the prayer time can be brief, such as three to five minutes.
- Provide the group with specific topics to guide their prayers for the pastor, or ask them to pray as they feel led.
- Encourage the prayer team members to have a reminder system for when to pray. For example, the participants can set a daily reminder on their smartphones.
- Whenever possible, have everyone pray at the same time, wherever they are, especially since the prayer time is brief.
- Repeat this intercessory prayer initiative at least once a year, if not more often. Most church ministries have a natural life cycle of three or four months. Our hope is that new participants will join each time.

Worship Service Prayer Team

Key Idea

The church's worship services are vital to the health and ministry of your church. More members gather then than at any other time in the life of the church. A prayer team can bring a God-centered revitalization to your services. The concept is simple: Three people pray in another room during each worship service.

Key Actions

- Designate a leader to coordinate this ministry.
- Select three people to pray for each worship service. Though it is always exciting when a lot of members want to participate in a ministry, we have found that limiting the number to three people praying for each worship service (even in larger churches) helps to build cohesion, focus,

and camaraderie in the group. As more people join the ministry, you can create a rotating schedule.

- Get members to commit to this ministry by signing up for it.
- Decide on a schedule for this ministry. It can be year-round or short-term, allowing breaks throughout the year. Some churches do four months on, two months off, four months on, two months off every year.
- Designate a separate room for the participants to gather in during the worship service.
- Give the participants the schedule or worship guide so they can pray for every specific aspect of the worship service. The participants can pray aloud or silently.
- If possible, provide the participants a way to see and/or hear the service in the prayer room.
- Remind the participants to pray especially for the pastor while he preaches.
- Tell the participants that if someone can't be present for a scheduled prayer time, he or she will be responsible for finding a substitute.
- Let the church know about this ministry. It may encourage others to participate in the future.

Adopt the Pastor's Family Members Prayer Ministry

Key Idea

One of the great challenges for many pastors is the stress placed on their family members. Pastors' families often feel as if they live in a fishbowl and must live up to unreasonable expectations. In this ministry, each family member of the pastor will have a specific prayer intercessor. Take the number of church members committed to the ministry and divide them evenly among the pastor's family members.

Key Actions

- Before you begin this prayer ministry, get the pastor's permission. He may want to discuss it with his family before giving the green light. Don't be discouraged if he prefers that this family member prayer ministry not be a part of the church's overall prayer emphasis. He may be concerned that it will exacerbate the fishbowl effect. Church members can still pray for the pastor's family without an organized ministry within the church.

- Designate a leader to coordinate this short-term ministry.
- Use as many communication venues as possible to get members involved.
- Get members to commit to this ministry by signing up for it.
- Plan an initial meeting—either in person or by videoconference—with those who have committed.
- Emphasize that the participants should not miss a day of prayer but that the prayer time can be brief, such as three to five minutes.
- Provide the group with specific topics to guide their prayers for the pastor's family, or ask them to pray as they feel led.
- If helpful and appropriate, have one designated participant per family member ask for prayer requests from that family member.
- Encourage the prayer team members to have a reminder system for when to pray. For example, the participants can set a daily reminder on their smartphones.
- Whenever possible, have everyone pray at the same time, wherever they are, especially since the prayer time is brief.
- If possible, repeat this family members prayer initiative at least once a year, if not more often. Most church ministries have a natural life cycle of three or four months. Our hope is that new participants will join each time.

About the Author

THOM S. RAINER is the founder and CEO of Church Answers, a former pastor, and bestselling author. With nearly forty years of ministry experience, Thom has spent a lifetime committed to the growth and health of the local church and its leaders. He is a 1977 graduate of the University of Alabama and earned his MDiv and PhD degrees from The Southern Baptist Theological Seminary. He and his wife live in Franklin, Tennessee.

Also from
Tyndale House Publishers
and Thom S. Rainer

Spend the next 30 days reaching
your community through prayer.

This simple yet powerful tool will help your
church members turn their focus outward and
experience the incredible power of prayer.

**It's easy. Anyone can do it.
Just pray and walk.**

DISCOVER WHAT IT REALLY MEANS TO BE A CHRISTIAN

Pastor, author, and church consultant Thom Rainer explains how you can find your true purpose within the community of fellow believers at your local church.

I Am a Christian: What does it really mean to be a Christian? In a world where everything from sports to politics, social media to podcasts, and movies to television competes for our attention, we need to get back to what is essential. When we finally grasp who we are in Christ and what our participation means to the local church, everything changes. Life begins to make sense. Our purpose becomes clear. Our mission through the local church is confirmed. Our hearts start longing to cooperate with God in the company of fellow believers.

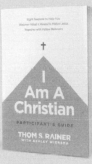

I Am a Christian Participant's Guide: This eight-week guide is designed to accompany Thom Rainer's *I Am a Christian DVD Experience*. Created for group or individual use.

I Am a Christian DVD Experience: In this eight-week video experience, Thom Rainer will help you and your small group dig deeper into what it really means to be a Christian and how your life will bloom when it's rooted in the local church.

CP1787

If you liked this book, you'll want to get involved in

Church Equip!

—

Do you have a desire to learn more about serving God through your local church?

Would you like to see how God can use you in new and exciting ways?

—

Get your church involved in Church Equip, an online ministry designed to prepare church leaders and church members to better serve God's mission and purpose.

Check us out at   **ChurchEquip.com**